THE *Youth Cybrarian's Guide*

to Developing
Instructional,
Curriculum-Related,
Summer Reading,
and
Recreational Programs

Lisa Champelli

Neal-Schuman Publishers, Inc.
New York   London

Published by Neal-Schuman Publishers, Inc.
100 Varick Street
New York, NY 10013

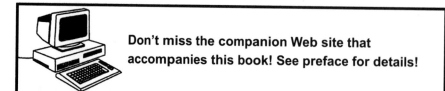

Don't miss the companion Web site that accompanies this book! See preface for details!

ISBN 1–55570–427–1

Dedication

To the talented, intelligent, creative, enthusiastic, and witty librarians with whom I work—especially the one whom I share my heart and home. You are daily inspiration.

Table of Contents

List of Figures

CHAPTER 3

CHAPTER 4

Foreword

By Carolyn Noah

The Internet is a baby on steroids, sprinting through its infancy to a pumped-up adolescence we couldn't have anticipated a few years ago. Youth librarians have responded to its development with an array of programming ideas incorporating its potential and addressing its challenges. Lisa Champelli captures their creativity in *The Youth Cybrarian's Guide to Developing Instructional, Curriculum-Related, Summer Reading, and Recreational Programs*.

Internet programming takes advantage of some happy coincidences. Among them are the insatiable interest kids have in things technological, the dynamic ways in which the Web supports curriculum, and the alluring interactivity that the Internet can bring to nearly any subject. Library Internet programming capitalizes on the synergy created by the technology with young people who learn by seeing, hearing, or doing.

The author has assembled information about a range of Internet programming that, to my knowledge, is unequaled in scope to date. She gathered programs of various types and for different ages, from instructive to creative. Along the way she incorporated information from some of the most notable libraries and librarians in the field. Samples come from school library media centers, and public library young adult and children's departments.

The best feature of this book is that each program is presented in the context of young people's developmental, social, or educational needs. With enough detail to make the programs replicable, Champelli reports on each program's target audience, Web site, goals, and the resources required to implement it. Included is a narrative so complete that in some cases the program is scripted. Many programs include screen captures and give a sense of the program's look and feel.

The book describes programs that can be accomplished with very little investment of staff time as well as some programs from large library settings where sophisticated equipment and specialized resources and personnel are available.

In essence, there's something within reach for every library setting.

Want to engage middle school students in using primary sources to learn about history? "Turn-of-the-Century Child Research Guide," reported by Debbie Abilock of The Nueva School in California, describes the development of an online curriculum taking advantage of the American Memory collection's free resources.

Looking for a no-fail way to capture teens' attention? Try following the model of Indiana's Monroe County Public Library's "E-Zine Workshop for Teens."

If you've ever struggled with ways to put public library summer reading programs on the Web, the chapter dedicated to reading programs is a treasure trove. Having worked with summer reading programs for years, I was excited by reading that chapter and recommend the book on that basis alone.

Also included are a variety of programs to adapt for teaching information literacy and Web page design.

Finally, an exhaustive section called "The Youth's Cybrarian's Source Box" provides dozens of additional starting points for the insatiable youth services programmer.

Use *The Youth Cybrarian's Guide* as a reference source or read it from cover to cover. Either way, expect to be tickled, teased, inspired, or driven to try one or more of these abundant ideas.

Preface

One of the most exciting aspects of a librarian's career is its continual state of change. Patrons come and go from season to season, new materials and equipment are added to the collection of informational resources; the very body of knowledge that the library strives to access is ever expanding. Of course, constant change is also one of the most frustrating things about working in libraries. Librarians are endlessly challenged to learn new skills while recalling the old, and to find innovative ways to integrate new materials and services into existing operating structures.

In the last decade, the vastly growing Internet, especially the World Wide Web, has been one of the new things that librarians have been required to learn to incorporate into daily services. While some librarians have resisted learning about yet another information medium, many more have embraced the Internet. The Children's Partnership recognized it as one of the new "information technologies rapidly transforming the way America operates and what our children need to learn" (1998). The Web-Based Education Commission calls it a "promising tool . . . with the power to expand the learning horizons of students of all ages" (2000).

According to the U.S. National Commission on Libraries and Information Science study, *Public Libraries and the Internet 2000*, 94.5 percent of public libraries provide public access to the Internet, up substantially from the 73.3 percent of public library outlets that provided public access to the Internet in 1998 (2000). The percentage of public libraries planning to implement or currently offering Internet access is near 100 percent.

The latest data of the National Center for Education Statistics (NCES) show the rapid rise in the percentage of public schools connected to the Internet. "By the fall of 2000, almost all public schools in the United States had access to the Internet: 98 percent were connected. In comparison, 35 percent of public schools had access to the Internet in 1994. In 1994, 3 percent of all U.S. public school instructional rooms were connected to the Internet (this includes classrooms, computer and other labs, library/media center, and any other room used for instructional purposes). By 2000, 77 percent were connected" (2001). Today all schools want to be wired to the Web.

Important questions come up for concerned professionals as these public schools and libraries recognize the importance of providing their patrons with Internet access. What have librarians been doing to teach people, specifically young people, about this new medium? How have librarians responded to youth interest in the Internet? How can librarians effectively utilize the power of the Internet and incorporate Web use in their library's instructional and recreational programs?

The Youth Cybrarian's Guide to Developing Instructional, Curriculum-Related, Summer Reading, and Recreational Programs displays some excellent examples of how youth service librarians in both school and public libraries have responded to their patrons' interest in and need to know about the Internet. These imaginative and inventive people have successfully integrated the use of the Internet, particularly the World Wide Web, into the library programs they conduct for children and young adults. *The Youth Cybrarian's Guide* illustrates many creative programming ideas with the inviting screen capture pictures of the Web pages that librarians have created or helped produce. The descriptions of these programs are designed to be complete enough so that other resourceful librarians (those who might not yet dare consider calling themselves "cybrarians") might be able to adapt and replicate them for use in their own libraries.

The Youth Cybrarian's Guide to Developing Instructional, Curriculum-Related, Summer Reading, and Recreational Programs has five major purposes:

- to provide arguments that promote the need for youth to have access to the Net;
- to recommend field-tested programs that support their access;
- to describe the ways youth service librarians have incorporated use of the Web in their programming for young people;
- to identify worthwhile and unique Internet applications being developed for kids;
- and to assemble Web resources librarians can refer to for their own continuing education purposes.

Gathering the innovative programming ideas detailed in this guide was a multi-faceted process. I began by writing about programs that I helped develop and conduct for the library where I work. I discovered others while searching for the best ideas in practical use today. I searched the Web for the school media centers and public libraries that had developed their own pages to teach children and young adults about the Internet, or which described curriculum-related or recreational programs that incorporated use of the Web.

I also posted announcements to the PUBYAC and LM-NET listservs inviting librarians to share their reports of how they have used the Internet in programs for children and young adults. The invitation requested that each report include a description of the program, the age level the program targets, why the librarian decided to offer this type of program, and the types of equipment needed.

Other librarians also referred me to colleagues they knew who had sponsored programs involving use of the Internet. I am extremely grateful to all the librarians who took time to describe their programs so that others might learn from their experiences and consider conducting similar activities. Quotes from these librarians (unless otherwise indicated) stem from e-mail messages and other correspondence we exchanged.

Librarians who have pondered how to teach young people about the Internet, or how to incorporate use of the Web into their library programs know what a time-consuming process it is to locate and review potential programming ideas, or develop a new one from scratch.

The Youth Cybrarian's Guide to Developing Instructional, Curriculum-Related, Summer Reading, and Recreational Programs does that investigative research for you. It is not a comprehensive listing of all the programs librarians have developed to teach young people about the Internet, or methods for integrating the Internet with traditional library services to children and young adults. Rather, it presents a great variety of intriguing programs to represent the tremendously creative and diverse kinds of excellent Internet programming youth service librarians across the country have developed. The programs are packaged and presented here as the type of insightful information one might gain from an experienced professional at a workshop or conference presentation.

No one can ignore the controversy often generated by the subject of Internet access and libraries. Since libraries started making the Internet available to their patrons, including children, hundreds of politicians and media reports have criticized the decision a majority of libraries have made to provide unrestricted Internet access. Their reports have spotlighted the types of unsavory materials found on the Internet, emphasized how unsuitable they are for minors, and accused librarians of failing to protect the welfare of children. This highly insulting accusation disregards the great care librarians have taken to teach Internet safety tips and to nurture the well-being of young people by developing their information literacy skills.

Shifting the focus away from the access controversy, this book spotlights librarians' efforts to guide and facilitate young people's use of the Net. *The Youth Cybrarian's Guide* investigates the engaging techniques that librarians use to teach children and young adults about the Internet and the safest, smartest ways to use it. It gives credit to the many efforts that librarians are taking to help children and young adults understand and effectively use Internet search tools. The guide also suggests resources librarians can use to help young people find and enjoy age-appropriate activities on the Internet.

The information contained in this book is organized as follows: Background Issues for Internet Programming reviews political efforts to limit youth access to the Internet and underscores the importance of remaining aware of legislation that may impact library services. It offers an assessment on the crucial relationship between librarians, youth, and the Internet and demonstrates the reasons why it is essential to teach children and young adults about the Internet.

Chapter 1, "Instructional Programs," presents creative programs and Web sites that public libraries have developed to teach children and their parents about the Internet and how to use it. It features the following programs:

- Monroe County Public Library's *Explore the Internet* program for children in grades 3–6 outlines points to cover when introducing young people to the Web. This introduction can be a great chance to inform school-age children of how the library's own Web site can help them locate great sites for kids.
- Milwaukee Public Library targeted parents when it developed both a Web-based tutorial and instructional classes to meet the Family Internet Training goal of its long-range plan.
- Carmel Clay Public Library employs a Power Point presentation in its *Internet Adventure* program to teach Internet searching skills to children in grades 4–6.
- Chicago Public Library conveys Internet safety tips to young people via a clever, interactive quiz it includes on its Web page for children and teens.
- The Akron-Summit County Public Library conducts a *College Information on the Web* program for young adults to familiarize college-bound students with the range of Web-based resources they can use to aid their college planning preparations.

Chapter 2, "Curriculum-Related Programs," describes interesting programs and Web sites developed by youth service librarians in school and public libraries for teaching children effective searching skills. It also features Web sites that librarians have developed to support curriculum-related research units. It includes the following programs:

- Heritage Middle School features librarian-selected search tools and pathfinders on the library's home page to help direct students to useful Web resources.

- The SearchQuest program at Springfield Township High School, developed for students in ninth grade and above, prompts students with questions to guide their evaluation of individual search tools and identify their special features. The outline for this program and other outstanding teaching tools are available on the Web.
- The students at The Ellis School learn to access the lesson on Internet search engines from a folder on the school computer network so that they can save their evaluations to the network for the librarian teaching the lesson to review.
- The *Turn-of-the-Century Child* program created at The Nueva School features resources from the Library of Congress that students can use to investigate their subject of study.
- Multnomah County Public Library's School Corps Web site and program help librarians provide Internet instruction to students in their schools.
- Librarians at Monroe County Public Library use their *What Would You Like to Know About Indiana?* Web site to introduce students to specific Web resources when they visit the library to conduct research about their home state.

Chapter 3, "Summer Reading Programs," profiles some of the exciting Web sites and methods librarians have created to enhance traditional summer reading programs for young people. It explores the following programs:

- Monroe County Public Library has designed quiz question games to appear on its summer reading Web site as an additional reading opportunity for children and a means for leading kids to related Web sites.
- In addition to providing summer reading activity sheets online, Multnomah County Public Library presents kids with the opportunity to register for the summer reading program via its Web site.
- Daughin County Library System employs creative graphic images and clever story lines to engage children in reading the mystery story it posts on its Web site.
- Carmel Clay Public Library incorporated trickster characters from folklore in its "Summer Story," which guided children on a Web Scavenger Hunt.
- Timberland Regional Public Library uses Web-based forms to communicate with children and young adults about what they are reading.

Chapter 4, "Recreational Programs," describes resourceful programs and Web sites that youth service librarians have developed that enable young people to use the Internet for creative expression or recreational exploration. It investigates the following programs:

- Dinosaurs and space are two perpetually popular topics that younger elementary-age children can explore on the Web easily via Monroe County Public Library's pre-selected links and guided programs.
- School-age students at Martin Library can investigate a variety of intriguing subjects through the Web sites librarians feature in *Cyber Camp* sessions.
- Children in grades 3–6 learn how to write HTML to create Web pages in Monroe County Public Library's *Web Design Workshop*.
- The *Web Design Class* for young adults at Ross Library employs Web page editing tools available through one of the free Web page hosting sites.
- Young adults participating in Monroe County Public Library's *E-Zine Workshop* get to determine the appearance and content of their magazine on the Web.

Chapter 5, "The Youth Cybrarian's Source Box," suggests Web sites that provide helpful tools to use when teaching young people how to use the World Wide Web, such as:

- Internet Safety Tips and Tutorials
- Search Tools
- Web Design Tools

The Source Box offers additional information on the following topics:

- Intellectual Freedom Issues and Filters
- WebQuests and Education-Related Sites
- List of Professional Association Web Sites and Listservs for Youth Librarians

The Source Box ends with a glossary that provides definitions of computer and Internet terms mentioned in this book, and refers readers to addresses of Web sites with additional material. These resources in the final chapter will help increase youth service librarians' knowledge and understanding of Internet issues, the tools required to develop Web pages and the places to go to learn more about integrating Web resources into library services. In general, the list of resources will provide librarians with the means to find additional information about the tools and topics discussed in each chapter and, overall, remain informed of changing technologies and policies concerning youth access to the Internet.

Visiting the Web sites is just a click away. You can easily access online the sites in each chapter, the Source Box, as well as the URLs included in the Chapter Notes and References on the companion Web site I have set up. Visit the *Youth Cybrarian's Guide* on the Web, available at: www.bloomington.in.us/~lchampel/ycg.html.

Please remember that the contributors to this book retain the copyright to their reports and complementary Web sites. They are described and depicted here for reference purposes only. Unless the creator of a Web site specifically grants permission for others to duplicate the images or information provided, you should always contact the creator before copying materials for your own use.

The Youth Cybrarian's Guide to Developing Instructional, Curriculum-Related, Summer Reading, and Recreational Programs promotes the outstanding efforts of librarians who care deeply about the welfare of young people and have dedicated library services to helping them to learn about the Internet and to use it most effectively.

The Internet has become a wondrous tool enhancing the lives of both librarians and the young people they serve. I hope exploring the work of other concerned, caring, and creative professionals will help you as you explore engaging programming ideas and create and use them in your own ever-changing library.

NOTES

Bertot, John C., and Charles R. McClure. 2000. *Public Libraries and the Internet 2000: Summary Findings and Data Tables* [Online]. Available: www.nclis.gov/statsurv/2000plo.pdf [29 September 2001].

Children's Partnership. 1998. *Children and New Technologies: Skills for the Future* [Online]. Available: www.childrenspartnership.org/pub/pbtc/part3.html#skills [29 September 2001].

National Center for Education Statistics. 2001. *Internet Access in U.S. Public Schools and Classrooms 1994-2000* [Online]. Available: http://nces.ed.gov/pubs2001/internetaccess/ [29 September 2001]. Also available at *NCES Fast Facts: Internet Access* (2001) [Online]. Available: nces.ed.gov/FastFacts/display.asp?id=46 [29 September 2001].

Web-Based Education Commission. 2000. *The Power of the Internet for Learning: Moving From Promise to Practice. Final Report* [Online]. Available: www.ed.gov/offices/AC/WBEC/FinalReport/Preface.pdf [29 September 2001].

Acknowledgments

The author is indebted to all of the librarians who graciously shared information about their programs and contributed material to this book. Many thanks to all listed in the final credits page for taking time out of their hectic schedules to document how and why they use the Web in the programs they conduct for children and young adults.

The author wishes to extend her gratitude to librarians Carrie Gardner, Coordinator of Library Media Services, Milton Hershey School, Hershey, Pennsylvania, and Carolyn Noah, Administrator of the Central Massachusetts Regional Library System, who shared her request for information with librarians in their service regions.

And a special thank you to these dedicated librarians and others who serve on the American Library Association's committees and round tables, working to define, promote, and teach the philosophies and practices of thoughtful librarianship.

Background Issues for Internet Programming: Children's Access to the Internet

Increasingly, people are expected to be not just literate but information literate, and studies have shown that access to or isolation from information resources have a major impact on a child's opportunities to succeed in the world today. Already, the Internet and the World Wide Web are part of our children's culture; tools they can use now for research, recreation, and communication, and in new ways that we have yet to imagine.

As members of the Web-Based Education Commission discovered:

> ". . . the Internet enables education to occur in places where there is none, extends resources where there are few, expands the learning day, and opens the learning place. . . . It connects people, communities, and resources to support learning. . . . It adds graphics, sound, video, and interaction to give teachers and students multiple paths for understanding. . . . The Web is a medium today's kids expect to use for expression and communication—it is the world into which they were born" (Web-Based Education Commission, 2000).

One mother, observing her young child's reading coaching session in the children's department of the public library where I work, remarked that occasionally when her daughter reads aloud she calls the punctuation at the end of a sentence a "dot-com" instead of a period. Whether or not children have regular access to the Internet, the popular culture of their era bombards their lives with the terms and images of the digital world. It seems, however, that more and more children do use the Internet regularly.

The National School Boards Foundation worked with Grunwald Associates, a leading market research and consulting firm specializing in technology, to develop a national survey of parents and children. Their report, *Children, Families, and the Internet 2000*, found that the number of children surfing the Internet in the United States has increased from 8 million in 1997 to 25 million in 2000. These figures represent 40 percent of American children 2 to 17 years old who use the Internet from either home or school, or both. The survey predicts the numbers of children using the Internet will likely increase to 70 percent, or 44 million children, by 2005. Of course, many children also have the opportunity to use the Internet in 95 percent of public libraries in the United States.

Most schools and public libraries across the country jumped at the chance to provide Internet access to their patrons, including children and young adults. They recognized that access to the Internet fit with some or all aspects of their service mission:

- to provide access to information
- to support educational activities
- to promote computer literacy and communication skills
- to sponsor recreational opportunities

As more and more Internet resources are being developed specifically for children, the benefits of Internet access for children continue to grow. And yet, so do the concerns. The Internet as a whole reflects the world as a whole and contains a range of offensive material we would prefer to avoid and not have children encounter.

The first national attempt to protect children from some of the more unsavory content distributed on the Internet was enacted by the U.S. Congress on February 1, 1996, in the form of the Communications Decency Act. The CDA intended to ban the transmission of obscene or indecent material across the Internet.

Recognizing that the vague provisions of the CDA threatened to undermine First Amendment rights to free speech, the America Library Association opposed the law. Its challenge was eventually consolidated in a suit brought by the American Civil Liberties Union (*ACLU v. Reno*). In a landmark decision issued on June 26, 1997, the Supreme Court ruled 7-2 that the Communications Decency Act was unconstitutional. Writing for the majority, Justice John Paul Stevens concluded: "As a matter of constitutional tradition, in the absence of evidence to the contrary, we presume that governmental regulation of the content of speech is more likely to interfere with the free exchange of ideas than to encourage it. The interest in encouraging freedom of expression in a democratic society outweighs any theoretical but unproven benefit of censorship" (Citizens Internet Empowerment Coalition, 1997).

After helping to defeat the CDA, the American Library Association and its Office for Intellectual Freedom concentrated on helping libraries evaluate different methods for managing public access to the Internet and ensuring that children have a positive experience online. While some libraries have responded to community pressures to install blocking and filtering tools on public access terminals, the American Library Association does not recommend the use of these tools. On July 2, 1997, the ALA Council adopted the *Resolution on the Use of Filtering Software in Libraries*, which resolved: "That the American Library Association affirms that the use of filtering software by libraries to block access to constitutionally protected speech violates the Library Bill of Rights."

On July 1, 1997, and again on November 17, 2000, ALA's Intellectual Freedom Committee issued a *Statement on Library Use of Filtering Software*. The Statement explains what blocking/filtering software is; the problems with the use of this software in libraries, and how libraries can promote access to the Internet. One of the methods the Statement suggests for promoting access to the Internet is to "Create and promote library Web pages designed both for general use and for use by children. These pages should point to sites that have been reviewed by library staff."

The first Children and Technology Committee of the Association for Library Service to Children, a division of ALA, did just that in 1997 when it compiled its list of *700+ Great Web Sites for Kids and the Adults Who Care About Them*. The same year, the Young Adult Library Services Association developed *TeenHoopla: An Internet Guide for Teens*. And in support of 1998–99 ALA President Ann Symons's campaign theme, "Celebrating the Freedom to Read! Learn! Connect!", ALA produced *The Librarian's Guide to Cyberspace for Parents and Kids* (1999) with selected sites for kids, safety tips, helpful information for parents, and more.

Despite the wealth of educational information produced by ALA, its committees and associations, debate about how best to facilitate youth access to the Internet continued to preoccupy professional, political, and public interest groups. While determining how best to prevent young people from being exposed to potentially harmful materials on the Internet was still a top priority for many, some agencies also were investigating how to prevent commercial entities from exploiting children and their rights to privacy.

In the summer of 1998, the Federal Trade Commission released a report, *Privacy Online: A Report to Congress*, which raised serious concerns about the privacy of children using the Internet. The report found that children often shared personally identifiable information about themselves and their families with commercial Web site operators as they played games, entered contests, communicated with online penpals, and filled out surveys. In response, Congress passed the Children's Online Privacy Protection Act (COPPA) in October 1998. The law (which didn't go into effect until April 21, 2000) requires certain commercial Web sites "to obtain parental consent before collecting, using, or disclosing personal information from children under 13" (Center for Media Education, n.d.).

While the American Library Association supported the law's efforts to regulate the abilities of certain commercial sites to *collect* personal information from children, it registered concern that the rules of the law actually inhibited the ability of children to communicate online. Commenting on the FTC's proposed rules for COPPA, the ALA, American Civil Liberties Union, and the Center for Democracy and Technology noted:

> "Under the Proposed Rule, Web sites that do not collect personal information from children will nonetheless be required to obtain verifiable parental consent before allowing children to participate in any service that allows children to speak. Simply put, any site that would enable a child to communicate with a peer, ask a question of a teacher, or e-mail to a neighborhood friend, would have to obtain parental consent before allowing such communications. For example, Internet sites that provide anonymous chat or e-mail services for children would be required to obtain parental consent, even if the operator of the site does not gather any information from the children" (American Civil Liberties Union . . . , 1999).

In fact, some commercial Web sites that provided free communication services, such as e-mail and chat rooms to kids had to discontinue those services because they couldn't afford to comply with COPPA's rules (Charny, 2000). Regrettably, this law, designed to protect children's privacy, also proved to inhibit their abilities to communicate online (Angwin, Tran, and Wingfield, 2000).

Although COPPA's regulations did not apply to libraries and their Web sites, libraries were indirectly impacted by COPPA. The American Library Association's Office for Information Technology Policy alerted libraries that they should be prepared to explain COPPA to children and their parents, as well as the greater community (American Library Association Office for Information Technology Policy, n.d.). At about the time that COPPA was passed, the National Commission on Libraries and Information Science was investigating how else the Internet was impacting libraries' services to children.

On November 10, 1998, the U.S. National Commission on Libraries and Information Science held a hearing titled *Kids and The Internet: The Promise and The Perils*. "Never before have students— of all ages—been able to gain so much access to information in support of their studies. But we also recognize what some have referred to as the 'dark side of the Internet.' . . . The Commission is especially sensitive to how these issues affect librarians," noted Jeanne Hurley Simon, NCLIS Chair (1999).

As an outcome of the hearing, the NCLIS issued practical guidelines to assist librarians and library trustees (or other governing bodies) in their efforts to manage children's access to the Internet. Recognizing that such management decisions must be local ones, based on the culture, customs, and character of each community, the Commission strongly recommended "that each library have a written 'acceptable use policy,' approved by its governing structure and reviewed periodically to adjust to the continuous changes in the Internet" (1999).

Just before the formation of the NCLIS hearings on *Kids and the Internet*, the United States Congress approved the Child Online Protection Act, in October 1998, in an effort to prohibit online sites from knowingly making available to minors material that is "harmful to minors (Electronic Privacy Information Center, n.d.)." Although the act itself was initially ruled unconstitutional, the congressionally appointed panel mandated by the act remained in place to "identify technological or other methods that will help reduce access by minors to material that is harmful to minors on the Internet" (COPA Commission, 2000).

In October 2000 the COPA Commission presented its final report to Congress. Its executive summary concluded that "no single technology or method will effectively protect children from harmful material online. Rather, the Commission determined that a combination of public education, consumer empowerment technologies and methods, increased enforcement of existing laws, and industry action are needed to address this concern" (2000).

Ignoring the recommendation issued by its own panel, and of NCLIS (which is charged with advising the executive and legislative branches on national library and information policies and plans), the United States Congress passed the Children's Internet Protection Act (CIPA) as part of a major spending bill signed into law on December 21, 2000 (Public Law 106-554). The Children's Internet Protection Act places restrictions on the use of funding that is available to libraries through various federally funded programs, including the Universal Service discount program known as the E-rate. In general, these restrictions require school and public libraries receiving federal funding for Internet access to install filtering software on all computers that offer Internet access. The law went into effect on April 20, 2001, but well before that date the American Library Association began efforts to protest it.

In January 2001, the American Library Association voted to initiate legal action challenging the Children's Internet Protection Act (CIPA), asserting the act is unconstitutional and creates an infringement of First Amendment protections.

"No filtering software successfully differentiates constitutionally protected speech from illegal speech on the Internet," ALA stated in the press release it issued announcing its decision to challenge CIPA (2001). The trial contesting CIPA was scheduled to start on March 25, 2002. In the meantime, ALA issued a number of advisories to libraries wondering how to comply with the law as they await the outcome of the trial. All are found on the American Library Association's CIPA Web site (available: www.ala.org/cipa/) (2000).

Throughout the whirlwind of controversies surrounding children's access to the Internet, librarians at school and public libraries across the country have quietly gone about their business of crafting policies and procedures for enabling all members of their communities to obtain access to Internet resources. While being attacked by well-meaning, but short-minded politicians, lobbyists, and zealous media personalities for providing unrestricted access to the Internet, librarians have been developing programs and Web sites to teach children and young adults about the Internet and how to use it wisely.

As part of its *Public Libraries and the Internet 2000* survey, the NCLIS found that

- 75.5 percent of public library outlets do not block and/or filter Internet content on their public access workstations
- 95.5 percent of public library outlets have acceptable use policies for their public access Internet services, and 43.6 percent differentiate between users (e.g., children, adults) in their policies
- 62.3 percent of public library outlets offer Internet training services, and 43.7 percent provide Internet training to children/youth

A survey conducted by Library Science professors Ann Curry and Ken Haycock for *School Library Journal* found that although more school libraries (53 percent) than public libraries (21 percent) use filtering software, approximately 96 percent of both school and public libraries have an Acceptable Use Policy, whether they filter or not, and 81 percent of both school and public libraries help guide their users' Internet searches by providing links to pre-selected Web sites and online research tools (Curry and Haycock, 2001).

These statistics can tell us about the numbers of libraries working to provide their communities with access to the Internet, teach their patrons about the Internet, and help guide their use. But the bare numbers don't illustrate *how* libraries are doing this. To learn how youth service librarians are teaching children and young adults about the Internet and incorporating Web-based resources into their programs, we need to speak to the librarians developing and implementing these services.

The following chapters present a snapshot of the valuable services librarians are providing to facilitate youth access to the Internet, including:

- General instructions on using the Internet and tips for smart, safe use
- Curriculum-related Web sites and instruction
- Web-based summer reading program activities
- Other recreational programs using the Web

The reports from the following librarians help us gain insight into what youth service librarians are doing to promote positive use of the Internet by young people, and why.

NOTES

American Civil Liberties Union, American Library Association, Center for Democracy and Technology. 1999. *Supplemental Comments to FTC's Proposed Rule Implementing the Children's Online Privacy Protection Act* [Online]. Available: www.ftc.gov/privacy/comments/supplementalcdtacluala.htm [29 September 2001].

American Library Association. 1997. *Resolution on the Use of Filtering Software in Libraries* [Online]. Available: www.ala.org/alaorg/oif/filt_res.html [29 September 2001].

——————. 1999. *The Librarian's Guide to Cyberspace for Parents and Kids* [Online]. Available: www.ala.org/parentspage/greatsites/guide.html [29 September 2001].

American Library Association, ALA Office for Intellectual Freedom and ALA Washington Office. 2000. *ALA's CIPA Web Site* [Online]. Available: www.ala.org/cipa/ [29 September 2001].

American Library Association Intellectual Freedom Committee. 1997, 2000. *Statement on Library Use of Filtering Software* [Online]. Available: www.ala.org/alaorg/oif/filt_stm.html [29 September 2001].

American Library Association News Release. 2001. *American Library Association Votes to Challenge CIPA* [Online]. Available: www.ala.org/news/v7n1/cipa.html [29 September 2001].

American Library Association Office for Information Technology Policy. n.d. *COPPA: The Children's Online Privacy Protection Act* [Online]. Available: www.ala.org/oitp/privacy.html [29 September 2001].

Angwin, Julia, and Khanh T.L. Tran, and Nick Wingfield. 2000. *COPPA Cost Too High for Some Sites* [Online]. *WSJ Interactive Edition*. Available: www.zdnet.com/zdnn/stories/news/ 0,4586,2554411,00.html [30 September 2001].

Bertot, John C., and Charles R. McClure. 2000. *Public Libraries and the Internet 2000: Summary Findings and Data Tables* [Online]. Available: www.nclis.gov/statsurv/2000plo.pdf [29 September 2001].

Center for Media Education. n.d. *Introduction to COPPA. A Parent's Guide to Children's Online Privacy: What Is COPPA?* [Online]. Available: www.kidsprivacy.org/whatis.html [29 September 2001].

Charny, Ben. 2000. *The Cost of COPPA: Kids' Site Stops Talking* [Online]. *ZDNet News*. Available: www.zdnet.com/zdnn/stories/ news/0,4586,2627742,00.html [29 September 2001].

Child Online Protection Act (COPA) Commission. 2000. *Final Report of the COPA Commission: Executive Summary* [Online]. Available: www.copacommission.org/report/executivesummary.shtml [29 September 2001].

Children and Technology Committee, Association for Library Service to Children. 1997. *700+ Great Web Sites for Kids and the Adults Who Care About Them* [Online]. Available: www.ala.org/ parentspage/greatsites/amazing.html [29 September 2001].

Citizens Internet Empowerment Coalition. 1997. [Online]. Available: www.ciec.org/ [29 September 2001].

Curry, Ann and Ken Haycock. 2001. *Filtered or Unfiltered?* [Online]. *School Library Journal*. Available: www.slj.com/articles/articles/ 20010101_9371.asp [29 September 2001].

Electronic Privacy Information Center. n.d. *Ashcroft v. ACLU (Formerly ACLU v. Reno II): The Legal Challenge to the Child Online Protection Act* [Online]. Available: www.epic.org/Free_speech/ copa/ [13 December 2001].

Federal Trade Commission. 1998. *Privacy Online: A Report to Congress* [Online]. Available: www.ftc.gov/reports/privacy3/conclu.htm [30 September 2001].

Grunwald Associates. 2000. *Children, Families and the Internet* [Online]. Available: www.grunwald.com/survey/survey_content.html [29 September 2001].

Stevens, John Paul. 1997. *Reno v. ACLU Decision* [Online]. *Electronic Privacy Information Center*. Available: www2.epic.org/cda/cda_decision.html#majority [29 September 2001].

U.S. National Commission on Libraries and Information Science. 1999. *Kids and The Internet: The Promise and The Perils. Practical Guidelines for Librarians and Library Trustees* [Online]. Available: www.nclis.gov/info/kids2.html [29 September 2001].

Web-Based Education Commission. 2000. *The Power of the Internet for Learning: Moving from Promise to Practice. Final Report* [Online]. Available: www.ed.gov/offices/AC/WBEC/FinalReport/Preface.pdf [29 September 2001].

Young Adult Library Services Association. 1997. *Teen Hoopla: An Internet Guide for Teens* [Online]. Available: www.ala.org/teenhoopla/index.html [29 September 2001].

REFERENCES

CNN Interactive. 1997. *Communications Decency Act Main Page* [Online]. Available: www.cnn.com/US/9703/cda.scotus/ [29 September 2001].

Edupage Editors. 2000. *Survey: Kids Fuel Internet Explosion* [Online]. Available: http://listserv.educause.edu/cgi-bin/wa.exe?A2=ind0006&L=edupage&D=1&H=1&O=D&F=&S=&P=437 [29 September 2001].

National School Boards Foundation. 2000. *Research and Guidelines for Children's Use of the Internet* [Online]. Available: www.nsbf.org/safe-smart/full-report.htm [14 October 2001].

Chapter 1

Instructional Programs

Organization after organization, agency after agency that has examined the question of how best to prevent children from being exposed to potentially harmful materials found on the Internet has emphasized that education is critical. Children and their parents need to understand what the Internet is and how to use it wisely.

Librarians can provide that type of instruction.

As the U.S. National Commission on Libraries and Information Science has stated, "Libraries can provide Internet training, education, and other awareness programs to parents, guardians and teachers that alert them to both the promise and the perils of the Internet and describe how children can have a safe and rewarding experience online" (1999).

And they have—libraries across the country have been providing this type of instruction and developing Web sites that guide children to appropriate resources and share tips for staying safe online. Some libraries' Web sites, such as the Seattle Public Library's children's services page on Internet safety links for parents and teachers, feature selected links to educational sites created by outside sources. One of the links included on Seattle's page, for example, is to "The Librarian's Guide to Cyberspace for Parents and Kids," developed by the American Library Association, which offers information for parents, safety tips, and a list of recommended Web sites for kids. Other libraries, such as the New York Public Library, have drafted their own Internet advice. NYPL's page states in part, "The best way to assure that your children are having a positive online experience is to stay in touch with what they are doing." Still other libraries are providing more active Internet instruction by developing topical library programs for their patrons. For example, in fall 2001, Appleton Public Library in Wisconsin advertised a three-part instructional series for students in grades four and up on the library's Family Internet Station. The first evening session explained basic concepts and functions of the Internet. The second session, the following week, familiarized students with the World Wide Web and search engines for locating sites. The third session discussed helpful reference books, research strategies, and how to use the magazine index to look up magazine and newspaper articles. Registration was required, and parents were welcome to attend the sessions too.

When is a child ready to learn how to use the Internet? Librarians interested in providing Internet instruction to young people have questioned what age level they should target. Certainly middle- and upper-elementary grade level students ask to use the Internet for homework assignments and to find recreational sites of interest to them. But often parents with children in kindergarten and first grade want their children to learn how to use the Internet. Is this a good idea? Sure—as long as the instruction is provided to both the parent and the child together in a shared instructional session. As the Children's Partnership states in its *Parent's Guide to the Information Superhighway*, "children [between the ages of four and seven] do learn intuitively and quickly, but at this age they still depend on parents for reading and interpreting directions" (1998). Younger children will certainly need help with typing in URLs and keywords.

Trying to use the Internet independently can be an exercise in frustration for children (or adults) who are novice readers. Beginning readers find it challenging to absorb the information presented on a Web page and figure out what to click on next, or to navigate through a hierarchy of subject headings in order to find their topic of interest. Even the third and fourth graders I work with ask for help spelling the search terms they want to use, or finding the instructions on a page that explain how to play a game.

Of course, a child's cognitive or developmental abilities do not necessarily correspond to a chronological age, but people proficient in the use of the Internet have found that independent use of the Internet is best suited to children in grades three and up. Walter Minkel, writing for *School Library Journal*, states, "All the research I've seen so far—such as the study reported in *SLJ* ('Does Not Compute,' July 2000)—suggests that kids under eight aren't really ready for the Internet. . . . And maybe the things that make the Internet so cool for older users—things like unstructured choice and the ability to hop from context to context—simply aren't developmentally appropriate for kids under third grade" (2001). The author of the book *Failure to Connect* reports that "Carol Baroudi, one of the authors of the ubiquitous *Internet for Dummies*, states firmly that children below age seven should not have unsupervised computer time. She considers eleven an optimal age for introduction to electronic communications" (Healy, 1998: 250).

Finding that adolescents are eager users of e-mail, chat, and other Internet communication tools, some libraries have concentrated on educating teens about how to use the Internet wisely. Susan Alatalo directs young adult services for Marlborough Public Library in Massachusetts. In 1999, Alatalo, who already had developed a handout of recommended Web sites for young adults and a bookmark listing online safety rules for kids, invited a detective from the local police department who works with youth services and a licensed psychologist familiar with studies of how the Internet impacts human relationships to present *Safe and Healthy on the Internet*, a program for teens, preteens, parents, and educators in her community.

As the reports in this chapter illustrate, there are a number of different types of Internet instruction programs a library might provide for its community. Some libraries have concentrated on sharing guidelines for online safety or have emphasized how to search for general information on the Internet. Other library Internet programs have focused on how to find specific information on the Net. Some have dedicated instruction to school-age students starting to learn research skills; others concentrate on educating parents, realizing that Internet-savvy parents will be able to assist and provide more confident supervision of their children's time online. Once you determine what age level you want to target, you'll need to determine what content to include.

In this chapter, I describe Monroe County Public Library's program, which provides a general introduction to the Internet and explains how to search for information on the Web, presented to children in grades three through six. The other libraries featured in this section share the different strategies they have developed for teaching young people about the Internet and how to use it effectively. These include:

- Milwaukee Public Library, Wisconsin
  Internet Tips for Parents Web tutorial and instructional program
- Carmel Clay Public Library, Indiana
  Internet Adventure for fourth through sixth grade students and parents
- Chicago Public Library, Illinois
  Internet Safety interactive Web site for children and teens
- Akron-Summit County Public Library, Norton Branch, Ohio
  College Information on the Web program for young adults

EXPLORE THE INTERNET—INTRODUCTION TO THE INTERNET FOR GRADES 3–6

MONROE COUNTY PUBLIC LIBRARY, INDIANA

CHILDREN'S SERVICES, www.monroe.lib.in.us/childrens/childrens_dept.html

Overview

Many of the children in Bloomington, Indiana, are fortunate to have Internet access in their homes, as well as from school and the public library. But does this mean they understand how to use the Internet? A third grader might be able to open a Web browser and click on a link, but does he understand how to find and retrieve information? Does she know what a search tool is and how to use it? Does he realize that the Internet contains a vast wealth of information, but not everything is on the Internet?

The *Explore the Internet* program aims to provide children with an overview of what the Internet is, how to navigate with a Web browser, and how to use a search tool to find and retrieve information on the World Wide Web. It also functions to introduce children to some of the Web resources that the children's librarians have developed to help them with their homework or find age-appropriate games to play.

This program was first offered to school-age children in 1997 when the library's new public computing center opened with 12 personal computers. The program's goals are to teach young people about the Internet and to let them know that the library's public computing center is a place for them. Although children are encouraged to search the Web from one of the three Internet computers located in the children's department, where a children's librarian can assist them, people of all ages are welcome in the public computing center and are able to use the Internet there to play, communicate, and find information of interest to them.

Program Title

Explore the Internet
www.monroe.lib.in.us/childrens/xplornet.html

Target Audience

This program is geared to children in third through sixth grade. Parents are welcome to observe from the back of the room if they wish, but the program is designed for kids to have a chance for hands-on practice using the Web on their own, under the supervision of the librarian conducting the program.
(*Reported by Lisa Champelli, children's librarian, Monroe County Public Library*)

Required Equipment

I initially conducted this program in MCPL's public computing center with 12 computers, sometimes asking the participants to share a computer so that more than 12 could take part. The PCC now contains 24 computers connected to the Internet. Participants have access to both Netscape and Internet Explorer Web browsers on their computers, but I ask them to please open whichever one I will be using so that we are all seeing the same thing. The computer I use is connected to a LitePro projector so that students can observe my demonstrations of different Web sites and tools, displayed on a screen at the front of the room. It is extremely helpful to have at least one other adult assist during the program.

Program Description

The Web page for this program basically serves as an outline to guide the content of the program, and as a reference source for patrons to use anytime. While the Web outline acts as a reminder for the different points I'd like to make, it truly functions as a guide; I don't follow it word for word. There is only so much you can cover in an hour and a half. Choose what to emphasize based on the skill level and interests of your participants.

Before the program, I make sure that links included in the outline are working, that the LitePro projector has been connected to the instructor's computer in the public computing center, and that the center's computers and any needed plug-in software are all functional. I also like to display both fiction and nonfiction books about the Internet on tables in the room and have any handouts ready for kids to take with them at the end of the program.

I post a sign on the outside door to the computing center alerting the public that the room will be closed for an hour and a half. (The manager of the public computing center also posts a calendar on the outside of the door so that people will have some advance notice as to when the center is unavailable for general use.) I ask children to register in advance for the program, but if there are still seats available, drop-in attendees are welcome.

Once everyone is seated, I like to welcome program participants to the library, let them know what room they are in, the purpose of the room, and that this is a place they can return to if they want to use the Internet again on their own.

I explain what the program will cover. It's important to let kids know that there will be plenty of time for them to try things out themselves, but there will also be times when I will ask them just to watch demonstrations on the screen at the front of the room. I assure them that they cannot break the Internet, encourage them to ask questions, and remind them that we are all still learning about the Internet and how best to use it.

Before I give my explanation of the Internet, I invite the kids to tell me what they think the Internet is. This helps me assess what the participants already know and presents a chance to dispel any misconceptions. I make sure they know the Internet is not just one computer, but many computers all over the world. These computers are connected to each other by phone lines or cables. All of these computers share a language in order to send information back and forth to each other. This language is called TCP/IP, which stands for Transmission Control Protocol/Internet Protocol. (I assure the kids they aren't going to be quizzed on anything, but I like to share the actual names for things when I can, so that the terms will be familiar when they hear them another time.)

I explain that there are different parts to the Internet and different ways to use it. Sending e-mail messages is one of the most popular ways to use the Internet. But in this program, we will focus on the World Wide Web, the part of the Internet that enables us to view words and pictures, watch movies and hear sounds, and link to different pieces of information.

Make sure that participants are all familiar with what a Web browser is and how to use it. Young people, like most people, are reluctant to admit they don't know how to do something, so this is a good place to ask them to watch on the screen as you point out the different parts of the Web browser that they should be familiar with.

Explain: In order to see World Wide Web pages, you have to have a kind of computer software called a Web browser. Internet Explorer and Netscape are both Web browsers that the MCPL uses. Let's look at Netscape today. There are some important buttons on the Netscape Web browser that can help you move around.

Home: Returns you to the homepage set at this computer.
Back: Moves you to the Web page you last visited.
Print: Lets you print the page you are looking at.

Another important part of the Web browser screen is the scroll bar on the right side. When you put the mouse arrow on this bar and then hold down the left button of the mouse, you can move the bar up or down. This lets you see more of the Web page you are on. You can also move up and down a Web page by clicking with the mouse arrow on the arrow boxes at the top and bottom of the scroll bar. Also point out that many Web pages can be moved up and down with the arrow buttons on the keyboard. (Some younger children who are still learning how to manipulate the mouse prefer using the arrows on the keyboard.) Explain that when you get to a new Web page, you usually only see a portion of the page in your computer screen. Because there's usually more information than what you see at first, it's generally a good idea to use the scroll bar or arrows to see all of the Web page to help you decide where to go or what to do next.

One of the most important parts of the Netscape screen is the Location window. This is where you can type in the addresses of Web pages that you would like to visit. Another name for a Web page address is a URL, which stands for Uniform Resource Locator. Every Web page address begins with the letters *http*. These letters stand for hypertext transfer protocol, which is the kind of computer language that permits Web pages to link together. The hypertext on a Web page that links you to another page is usually blue and underlined, but the sure way to tell whether a word or picture is a link to another page is to move the mouse arrow over that word or picture. If the arrow changes into a hand, you know you can click on that word or picture to link to another page.

In addition to giving kids tips for how best to search for information on the Internet, the program touches on safety issues and how to be smart about using the Internet. I think it's important to caution children that sometimes when people search the Web, they come across things they didn't expect or want to find. If they find themselves at a Web site they didn't expect to get to, or if they are confused about how to get out of a Web site they don't want to visit, I assure them that they can *always* come to a librarian for assistance when they are in the library.

When alerting kids that they might encounter images or information that they didn't expect to see, we used to be able to tell them to click on the home button or the "X" button at the top right of the Web browser to start over or end their session. But in the last year, librarians have discovered Web sites that have been designed to open second and third and succeeding Web browsers with the same annoying site when the user attempts to leave the site by either of these methods. So although we still suggest these methods as ways for exiting an unwelcome site, we make a point to tell kids that they can always come to librarians for help. I feel that children are less alarmed by something when they know they can take some action and do something about it, and I like to remind them, "When you're using the computer, you are the one in control. You get to decide where you want to go and what you want to read and view."

Next, we take a look at how to connect to a specific Web page.

Explain: When you know the address of a certain Web page—maybe you found a URL in a book or magazine or newspaper article, or your friend told you about a cool site that you want to visit—all you have to do is type the address in the Location window on the Web browser. First click with the mouse in the window.

I demonstrate how to delete or backspace over the address that is already there and I advise them to type the address exactly as it is printed. For practice I ask the class to type "http://www.bonus.com."

Billed as a "SuperSite" for kids, I feature this site because it is now home to Beakman and Jax, cartoon characters who answer science-related questions. There are a number of terrific interactive demos, including one of the best sites I have seen for illustrating how information is sent across the Internet. (You can also find some good animations of how different elements of the Internet work depicted on "The Animated Internet" pages from the Learn the Net Web site, www.learnthenet.com/english/animate/animate.htm.) Beakman and Jax's interactive demo does require the Shockwave plug-in, so you might want to avoid it if you don't want to install Shockwave.

To find this demo on bonus.com, click on the menu heading for "Brains." Beakman and Jax appear in the directory. Click on their picture and then select the "Beakman and Jax" heading on the next page for a complete listing of all their activities. Click on the link for "Interactive Stuff" then scroll down until you see a link for "How Does the Internet Work?" (also www.beakman.bonus.com/beakman/interact/demo.html).

Ask kids to type a short message to Beakman, click on the "Send Mail" button and watch as the message is broken down into separate packets to be transferred through the telephone lines. Beakman types an automatic message back to the sender. Demonstrate to the kids how the storm clouds on this site can knock down telephone lines, and watch how messages can be rerouted and find another way to get to their recipients. (Most kids enjoy sending and receiving messages and trying to "break" the Internet, so determine how much time you have for this activity, and let kids know they can come back to this page later if they want!)

If you'd rather not hassle with Shockwave, choose another site that kids will appreciate, preferably one with a short address, such as www.zeeks.com.

Next, I ask the kids how they can get to a Web site when they don't know its address. I agree that, yes, sometimes you can guess a Web site's address (like pokemon.com), but I don't encourage this because sometimes the address is for something completely different! (Note: Because of the advances in Web browser capabilities, many kids think they can type the word that they want into the Location window of the browser and the site they are looking for will appear.) First, I suggest they check the children's services Web site to see if we have linked to a game or to a homework helper site they might like. If they can't find a direct link from the children's services page, then they should use an Internet search tool.

I show them how to find search tools from the children's services homepage and briefly discuss the difference between a subject directory like Kids Click (http://sunsite.berkeley.edu/KidsClick!/) and a search engine like Webcrawler (www.webcrawler.com) by explaining that a subject directory usually has a person who reviews the sites to be included in the directory and that the search engine relies more on a computer "robot" to look for sites to be included in its directory. The computer robot can usually work faster and gather more sites, but the human reviewer usually has more accurate or more relevant sites in its directory, although not as many.

I point out that both kinds of search tools usually have a search window where you can type in the keywords for the subject you are looking for, as well as a directory where you can click on the topic headings that lead to your specific subject. I have found that many younger children are impatient with the number of clicks they have to make on directory headings to find what they want, so we practice choosing keywords and entering them in the search window. I suggest they look for information on tornadoes, but give them the option of searching for a topic of their own choosing.

I don't discuss advanced searching techniques much in this program. I might demonstrate how to limit a search by putting quote marks around a phrase, but for children at this age, I emphasize using the search tools designed for kids and concentrate on helping them choose good keywords. I also try to leave a little time to discuss reviewing the information they find on the Web: the importance of being careful readers of Web pages, looking for an author, and paying attention to the Web page's address to help figure out where the information is coming from and whether it contains information you can trust.

I explain what the different domain name endings mean:

www.bonus.com (.com = commercial enterprise)
www.pbs.org (.org = organization)
www.indiana.edu (.edu = educational institution)
www.nasa.gov (.gov = government agency)
www.monroe.lib.in.us (.us = region: United States)

I also like to point out to kids that many Web sites contain advertisements, or commercials, just as we find commercials on television. Although these ads sometimes look like games to play, they are usually trying to sell you something, or direct you to another Web page. We also discuss the importance of not giving out personal information, such as last name, home address, or phone number, on a Web site.

It would be very easy to extend the length of this program to explain in greater detail safety tips, search techniques, and how to evaluate the results of a search, but it's important to allow time for kids to practice using different search tools. At this point, I encourage the participants to think of a topic that they would like to learn more about and try finding information about that topic on the Web using one of the Internet search tools. If you have a printer available, you might also demonstrate how to print a page from the Web. Nothing helps to instill a greater feeling of "ownership" than enabling kids to take home a printout of the information they found.

While kids are conducting their own searches, walk around the room to help when they get stuck, to answer questions, and to observe their discoveries! A few minutes before the program concludes, let them know they should finish what they are doing. As children are leaving, give them each a handout with the address, phone number, and hours of the library, along with the URL for the library's Web page, or of the page you used in the program, or for a favorite search tool, so that they will be able to continue their exploration on their own another time.

Insights & Improvements

I used to have the Web browsers open at each computer and encouraged the kids to explore on their own while they were waiting for the program to start. But once I was ready to start the program, it was sometimes difficult to get everyone to stop using the computer to listen and to watch what I was doing. Now I give each child a word find puzzle when they come in and ask them to find Internet vocabulary words while we wait for the program to begin. (I've used the Word Find Puzzle Builder, http://kids.msfc.nasa.gov/Teachers/WordFindBuilder/PuzzleBuilder.html.)

Conducting this program often involves finding the balance between allowing kids the maximum amount of time for independent exploration and keeping them focused on the topic at hand. I have found that 20 minutes usually is sufficient for "free time" because many kids quickly find a game to play and are content to stick with that activity until the end of the program. For future programs, I plan to revise the Web page to condense the text, increase the type size, and make it easier to use overall.

To help kids think about the different ways they can find information on the library's Web site, and to encourage them to try using different search tools, I sometimes include an "Internet Treasure Hunt" as part of this program. Before the program starts, I make sure that I can still find all the answers to the questions posed on the Internet Treasure Hunt page (www.monroe.lib.in.us/childrens/treasurehunt1.html), revise any questions that need to be updated, and then print out the page to give to program participants so they'll have some place to record their answers. When I promote this program as a "Homework Help on the Web" workshop, I also show participants where they can learn how to cite online sources.

If kids ask if they can go to the Pokemon homepage, or to another site whose address they have memorized, I'll ask them to try out the search I've suggested first, since one of the objectives of the program is helping kids learn how to find unknown Web sites that may be useful to them. But as the program title indicates, they're encouraged to explore and return to their favorite sites if they like. While I expect that they will learn something useful from the program and leave knowing more about the Internet than when they came in, my ultimate goal is for them to feel comfortable using the Web, to feel good about visiting the library, and to remember that the library is a place they can come to find all kinds of information, complete with librarians to help them!

Contact Person

Lisa Champelli, Children's Librarian
Monroe County Public Library
303 East Kirkwood Avenue, Bloomington, IN 47408
lchampel@monroe.lib.in.us

INTERNET TIPS FOR PARENTS—WEB TUTORIAL AND INSTRUCTIONAL PROGRAM

MILWAUKEE PUBLIC LIBRARY, WISCONSIN

www.mpl.org/

Overview

Family Internet training was a goal in Milwaukee Public Library's 1998-1999 long-range plan. In 1998, Milwaukee Public Library (MPL) and Milwaukee Public School (MPS) were awarded an Educational Technology Training & Technical Assistance Grant from Technology for Educational Achievement (TEACH) in Wisconsin.

The TEACH grant, explains Leah Raven, grant project coordinator, sought to enhance and expand services to Milwaukee residents by melding the technological savvy of MPS high school students with the technology and training needs of MPL, its patrons, parents of MPS students, and other members of the community. Developed by Lynn Bellehumeur, MPL's technical services head, in conjunction with the Milwaukee Public School, the main goal of the grant was to provide Milwaukee residents with computer services through the development of four library service areas:

- Hiring of computer service aides
- Providing public training sessions
- Offering staff training sessions
- Constructing a computer lab at one of the neighborhood libraries.

Although each service area plays a key role in helping to educate Milwaukee parents and other community members about the Internet, the largest component of the TEACH grant was the development of the free public training sessions. The following report describes the creation of the library's *Internet Tutorial* Web site and how MPL conducted its public training sessions. Is it possible to develop such a program without the aid of additional financial and human resources that a grant award can provide? Yes, but grant funding certainly does help. There's no denying that coordinating a comprehensive Internet instruction program like this one requires dedication of staff time. Librarians must, at the very least, have scheduled

Figure 1-1: Homepage for the Milwaukee Public Library's Web tutorial *The Internet: Tips for Parents*

time to plan such a program and familiarize themselves with the tools they will use to conduct an instructional program that educates patrons about computer and Internet resources.

Raven notes that "with staff shortages due to a hiring freeze, having an extra person (a grant project coordinator) to research Web resources for families, develop the tutorial, plan train-the-trainer sessions, and handle part of the registration for the sessions allowed the project to move forward. It was also helpful to have extra funds that could also be used for promotional materials and supplies. I was really pleased with the final version of the Web tutorial, and as you can see it was a joint project by many MPL staff."

Program Title

Internet Tips for Parents
www.mpl.org/files/kids/intro.htm

Target Audience

Parents of elementary school-age children
(Reported by Leah Raven, grant project coordinator, in collaboration with Paula Kiely, deputy city librarian; Linda Vincent, automation librarian; Susan Pack, training coordinator; Lynn Bellehumeur,

technical services head; and children's librarians Kelly Hughbanks, Susan Knorr, Kathie Staszak, and Cynthia Wagner.)

Required Equipment

The presentations were given at the central library and at all 12 neighborhood libraries in the city of Milwaukee. Hands-on sessions were conducted at locations with computer labs. Computer labs vary in size (anywhere from 8 to 12 computers) and allow for an LCD projector to be set up so patrons can follow along with the trainer. At locations where there was not a lab, presentations were given in the meeting room where a computer and projector were set up and the audience was simply given a demonstration. (At the time of the Family Internet program, we had six Sharp MV2 LCD projectors that were used for both hands-on and demonstration sessions.)

The tutorial really only required the use of a Web browser. However, MPL has a number of computer applications installed on workstations within the libraries, including Netscape, Microsoft Word, Microsoft Excel, and Ainsworth Keyboard Trainer, along with a multitude of electronic resources and subscription databases. The library also has a different configuration for the children's computers, which provide a host of educational software applications.

Although we have a large number of plug-ins (media players, file viewers for images, Acrobat Reader, and so on) installed on library computers, they were not required for running the tutorial. Because we wanted to allow patrons to access it from home, we made a concerted effort to keep the tutorial simple and allow for easy accessibility and navigation.

Program Description

I became involved with the Family Internet Web Tutorial project in the summer of 1999. At the time, I was coordinating two grants at the Milwaukee Public Library, both involving developing curriculum and developing public computer training sessions. At that time, Paula Kiely, who was the children's services coordinator (she is currently the deputy city librarian) approached me about a project the children's librarians had been working on. They wanted to develop an online presentation that could be used in one-hour training sessions geared toward parents of elementary school-age children who were not familiar with computers or the Internet.

The children's librarians at the Milwaukee Public Library recognized that most children who were using the library were comfortable using computers and the Internet. They freely explored Web sites and learned new things on their own. However, many parents of these children considered themselves to be "computer illiterate." They were hesitant to explore the Internet without instruction. *The Internet: Tips for Parents* Web tutorial was developed as a tool to introduce and guide parents through basic computer and Internet searching skills.

I was given an outline of specific topics the children's librarians would like to include. This was an incredible opportunity for me, because I had been wanting to create my own Web tutorial for some time, especially after teaching Internet classes for library patrons who were at a very beginning level, and also after my previous experience training business clients at a for-profit training center in the area.

I spent quite some time looking at other tutorials, evaluating what worked and what did not. I put together several drafts of the tutorial and met with Paula Kiely and Kelly Hughbanks, a children's librarian, for their input throughout the summer of 1999. We decided that the language used would be simple and not too technical. We would try to limit the amount of text per page because it would be used in a presentation. However, there would be a sufficient amount of information for those going through the tutorial on their own. (There would be established goals and objectives for what this Web tutorial hoped to achieve, scroll bar practice as well as a "find the hyperlink" exercise). The table of contents could be a jumping-off point so the librarian conducting the training session could modify the presentation based on the attendees' questions or skill levels. We also wanted to be sure to include links to other Internet resources that both parents and their children would benefit from, enjoy, and use.

Kelly Hughbanks provided the glossary of terms. Linda Vincent, the automation librarian, helped find Web resources and offered suggestions on Web content, and Susan Pack, the training coordinator, helped with editing.

After several drafts, I met with the graphic artist at MPL, Mary Slough, who worked on design and layout elements, the main graphic on the opening page, the page headers, and the images used on each page to illustrate the concept or terms being defined

At the end of the summer, I met with all the children's librarians involved with this project (Paula Kiely, Kelly Hughbanks, Susan Knorr, Kathie Staszak, and Cynthia Wagner) in a train-the-trainer session to go through the Web tutorial and suggest ways to present the material, and to modify the Web content with their suggestions. These five librarians then went out to the neighborhood libraries and presented the program.

GOALS

Our goal was to educate parents in the use of a Web interface, demonstrate simple strategies in exploring the Internet with their families, and provide a sampling of how they could use these electronic resources to help their children with homework or for their own use.

The specific goals of the program, as stated in the tutorial, are:

- Heighten parents' awareness of the Internet—its possibilities and its problems.
- Provide parents with guidelines for safe surfing.
- Demonstrate how families can use the Internet together as an educational tool, a rich resource of information, and a way to communicate with family and friends.
- Create awareness of Milwaukee Public Librarians as Internet navigators and as an ongoing resource for parents and families.

The following objectives will help us realize the goals of *The Internet: Tips for Parents* Web tutorial:

- Provide instruction on computer basics (including using the mouse, identifying parts of the window, and using scroll bars, toolbars, and hyperlinks).
- Familiarize parents with Netscape Navigator Web browser and the Milwaukee Public Library Web site.
- Explore ways parents can locate quality Web sites and access online resources (such as e-mail, listservs, newsgroups, and chat rooms).
- Provide tips for evaluating Web sites, explain safe surfing, and offer guidelines parents can implement for children's Internet use.

The outline presentation is not only useful as a guide when presenting the program to a group, but it can also be used independently by anyone who would like to learn more about using the Internet. The outline format allows patrons to pick and choose what they would like to learn. There is no need to follow the tutorial from start to finish. In this way they can concentrate on what is of most interest to them.

Insights & Improvements

The Web tutorial was used as a program outline for the one-hour presentation. The audience was polled at the beginning of the presentation to determine their computer navigational skills and their reasons for attending. The presenter would then tailor the presenta-

Figure 1-2: Table of Contents page (www.mpl.org/files/kids/tutorial.htm)

Internet Tips for Parents

Click on a topic that interests you, or click the "next" link at the bottom of this page to enter the web tutorial. The table of contents link at the bottom of every page will always take you to this page.

Introduction
- Goals of the Program
- Objectives of the Course
- Pretest: Are you a Newbie?

What is the Internet?
- Internet Defined
- Parts of the Internet
- World Wide Web
- E-mail
- Free E-mail Providers
- Listservs
- Newsgroups
- Chat Rooms

Online Tips
- Evaluating Web Sites
- Netiquette: Rules of the Road
- Privacy and Security
- Safety Tips
- Guidelines for Parents
- Library Internet Policy

Navigation
- Using the Mouse
- Scroll Bars
- Hyperlinks
- Hyperlinks Practice
- You've Found the Hyperlink
- Interface
- Toolbars

Locating Information
- Links on the MPL Web Site
- Web Addresses
- Searching for Info
- Search Tools for Kids
- Advanced Searching

Resources
- Internet Access
- Library Resources
- Online Resources for Parents
- Great Family Web Sites
- Internet Quiz
- Internet Quiz Answers
- Glossary of Terms

back | next

Milwaukee Public Library's "The Internet: Tips for Parents" web tutorial was created with funding provided by a TEACH Wisconsin Technical Assistance and Training grant. TEACH Wisconsin

MILWAUKEE PUBLIC LIBRARY

814 W. Wisconsin Ave. Milwaukee, WI 53233 (414) 286-3000
Send comments regarding this website to Webmaster@mpl.org
Last updated:Tuesday, September 28, 1999

tion to the skill level and interest of the audience, spending more time on the most appropriate areas.

In locations that have computer labs, the presentation is hands-on and time is incorporated during the session for participants to practice new skills and follow along with the presenter. At libraries without computer labs, the presentation includes a lecture in the meeting room for 30 to 45 minutes, followed by time for each person to use the computers that are available to the public throughout the library.

We found that one hour was not enough time for most participants, and the programs ran longer, sometimes up to two hours. For participants who chose to stay longer, there was always time after the initial hour to use the computers and ask questions.

The hands-on presentations were found to be the most effective. Many parents needed help with some basics, such as using the keyboard and mouse. Although one-hour sessions were planned for these introductory presentations, our experience showed us that a two-hour program would allow for more questions and answers and more hands-on time.

Contact Person

Lorelei Starck, Communications Director
Milwaukee Public Library
814 West Wisconsin Avenue
Milwaukee, WI 53233
(414) 286-3032
lstarc@mpl.org

INTERNET ADVENTURES FOR FOURTH THROUGH SIXTH GRADE STUDENTS AND PARENTS

CARMEL CLAY PUBLIC LIBRARY, INDIANA

www.carmel.lib.in.us/

Overview

Jennifer Andersen, children's librarian at Carmel Clay Public Library, developed an Internet instruction program for children and parents at her library after attending a presentation given by Librarian Carroll Davey at the 1999 American Library Association's annual conference. Head of Children's Services for Evergreen Branch, Jefferson County Public Library, Colorado, Davey described the Internet instruction program she conducts. (Davey's outline is on the Web at http://info.jefferson.lib.co.us/ala99/notes.html. Schools and public libraries may reproduce her materials for use with their own patrons.)

Andersen's program is geared toward elementary-age students, but like the Milwaukee Public Library, she also has found that it is the parents who most need the training, especially for learning how to help their children with homework. Andersen presents this program using PowerPoint slides as a visual aid, partly because that's how she first saw this instructional program presented, and partly so that she can change and edit the slides as needed. If she were to create a Web page to use in the program, she would need to rely on staff in the computer technology department to update the page whenever she made revisions to the program.

Program Title

Internet Adventure

Target Audience

Students in grades four through six, accompanied by a parent or caregiver. (*Each* child must have a parent or caregiver in attendance. If two siblings attend, then two parents or caregivers must attend.) (*Reported by Jennifer Andersen, children's librarian*)

Required Equipment

This program is conducted in the CCPL computer training room, which contains ten trainee computers, one instructor computer, and a screen. All the computers are connected to the Internet through a T1 line. We hook up an LCD projector to the instructor's computer so participants can view the instructor's screen. A VCR is also connected to the LCD projector.

The Netscape Navigator Web browser and PowerPoint presentation software are the only software applications used.

This program is run using two staff members, one as the instructor and the other as a helper in the room to aid participants as needed.

Program Description

GOALS

1. Introduce the Internet to children in grades four through six and their parents, so they can more effectively and safely search the Internet at the library and at home.

   - Introduce Netscape and its toolbar buttons and their functions.
   - Identify basic Internet terms and briefly introduce its history so children and parents can better understand how the Internet works.
   - Introduce Boolean searching so children and parents can conduct better Internet searches and receive the information they need for school reports.

- Introduce questions to aid children and parents in evaluating Web sites so children can determine which sites have valuable, accurate information.
- Introduce books in our print collection about computers, the Internet, and e-mail via a distributed bibliography.
- Introduce the library's Web site and children's department Web site, especially the Homework Help Page, so children and parents are more familiar with library resources.

2. Introduce tips for safely exploring the Internet.

FORMAT

I adapted the outline from Jefferson County Public Library, Colorado, to fit our library's resources and needs. I use PowerPoint slides for the presentation because I am constantly revising the program and I need to be able to change the slides when necessary. This format also allows me to run the program if the Internet goes down. That hasn't happened yet, but our programs are scheduled in the evenings after the staff of the computer technology department has gone home for the day, so if something did happen, it might not be fixed in time for the program.

Parents sit with their children at the computer during the *Internet Adventure* program to help with spelling and searching and to see what their kids are learning in the class.

During the first part of the class (about 15 minutes), the instructor briefly covers the Internet's history and how it works. The instructor then goes on to discuss Netscape and its toolbar.

The second part of the class (about 30 minutes) covers search engines, how to create a search using Boolean logic, and Web site evaluation. Using a Dry Erase board, the instructor shows how to do a search for information on the red fox. The instructor then has the participants choose a search engine and actually do the red fox search. At this time, the instructor and helper move around the room, answering questions and giving advice. Once everyone has found some relevant information about the red fox, the instructor and participants compare results and discuss whether or not they would be appropriate to use for a homework assignment.

The third part of the class (about 15 minutes) covers Internet safety. This part includes a short six-minute video, *Internet and Street Smarts* (1998), which was produced by two former FBI agents in cooperation with Nagy Film & Video. The instructor also discusses types of books available in the library for further study, and encourages parents to use preselected sites and the CCPL Children's Homework Help Page (www.carmel.lib.in.us/child/chlinks/homework.cfm) as starting points.

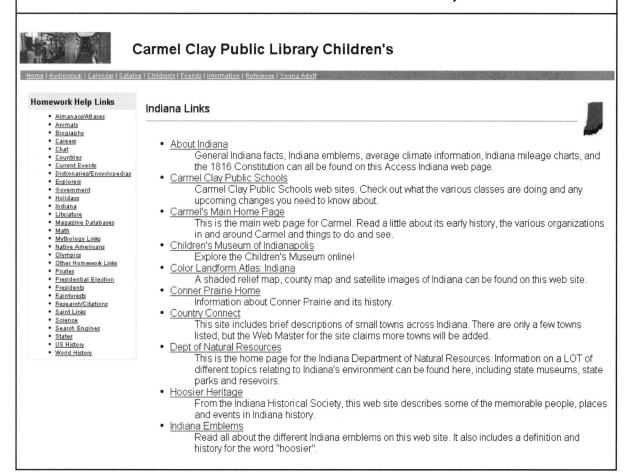

Figure 1-3: Carmel Clay Public Library's Homework Help Links for Children includes a listing of sites for state and local information (www.carmel.lib.in.us/child/chlinks/homework.cfm?linksub=indiana).

During the final part of the class (about 15 minutes), the participants are given a chance to practice searching. The instructor gives the participants a couple of questions, asking them to deduce the search terms, and the participants use the search engine of their choice. This gives the instructor and helper a chance to answer specific questions and provide individual attention.

Insights & Improvements

This program needs to be interactive, otherwise the participants get bored. Originally the class was set up to have all the participants do exactly the same red fox search on the same search engine. To allow participants the chance to use a search engine with which they are already familiar, we ask them to choose a search engine. This reinforces concepts discussed earlier in the class (our Homework Help

Page search engine links, as well as the search button on Netscape).

Participants need time to apply the search tips covered. Based on participant evaluations, we added more practice time to the end of the class. Participants were encouraged (but not required) to stay. In the future this practice time will include a worksheet that participants can use to practice either at the end of class or at home.

Covering the basics (history, how the Internet works, Netscape buttons) is necessary, as we have participants with a wide variety of experience, but too much is overwhelming. We shortened this part of the class to allow more time for Internet searching.

Many of our patrons immediately go on the Internet to find information for their homework assignments. Often a book or encyclopedia article would fit their needs better. I hope to make the class into a "how to do research" class that includes Internet searching, CD-ROM encyclopedias, InfoTrac, and our Homework Help page.

Contact Person

Jennifer Andersen, Children's Librarian
55 Fourth Avenue SE
Carmel, IN 46074
(317) 844-3363
jandersen@carmel.lib.in.us

INTERNET SAFETY—INTERACTIVE WEB SITE FOR CHILDREN AND TEENS

CHICAGO PUBLIC LIBRARY, ILLINOIS

www.chipublib.org/

Overview

Most libraries find themselves begging for a little name recognition and publicity. But being proclaimed by Family Friendly Libraries and the now defunct Filtering Facts organization as one of the ten most unsafe public libraries for children is the kind of publicity we all could do without. Chicago Public Library appeared tenth on the list (released September 1999) for its Internet use policy stating that "It is

Figure 1-4: The Chicago Public Library's homepage for kids and teens features an Internet Safety game to play (www.chipublib.org/008subject/003cya/sign/sign.html).

not within the purview of the Library to monitor access to any resource for any segment of the population." In agreement with the American Library Association's Intellectual Freedom positions, the statement is actually a recommended policy for libraries that do not act *en loco parentis*, or in place of a parent.

But when these inflammatory organizations proclaim to Dr. Laura and other talk show hosts how awful certain libraries are, they neglect to publicize all the efforts Chicago Public Library and others have taken to teach young people about the Internet and how to use it in a smart and safe manner. On its homepage, CPL's link to "Kids and Teens" leads to the attractively designed "Sign of the Owl" Web page. Links on this page include "Good Things on the Web," "Homework Help," and "Good Reads and Great Books." The top link on this page is titled "Internet Safety." The following report describes the Chicago Public Library's Web site for kids and teens, particularly the interactive Internet Safety section.

Program Title

Sign of the Owl: Internet Safety
www.chipublib.org/008subject/003cya/sign/sign.html

Target Audience

Different audiences are targeted within the pages, children ages 5 to 12, teens ages 12 to 18, and adults, with different sections for parents, teachers, and youth service librarians.
(*Reported by Cindy C. Welch, young adult specialist*)

Required Equipment

A computer with Internet access and a Web browser. The site requires Java, and we're starting to use Shockwave.

Program Description

Even though I'm describing a Web site section and not a program, we do have a philosophy in developing the Sign of the Owl. We do not believe in taking a reactive approach to Web use (filtering). We prefer to use a proactive approach, providing youth with Web sites that will draw their attention and keep them from jumping off our pages and onto questionable sites. Each site listed in this section has been screened by a librarian, sometimes by two or more.

Our second purpose in assembling this information is so that it is immediately useful for homework assignments—useful to children and to reference librarians. Often, there is little time to try to find material on the Web when many are waiting to be served. We wanted to discourage general site bookmarking in individual libraries when we could assemble pages of useful links that many people might be seeking. There is a small amount of original content, primarily in the form of artwork and book lists. The artwork lets us customize our Web site and give it a look unique to the Chicago Public Library, and the book lists provide reading suggestions for all ages. At different times of the year we feature certain departmental programming. For example, we create specific sections for our summer reading program. (See the Chicago Public Library *Reading Is Art-Rageous* summer reading program 2001 site, www.chipublib.org/003cpl/childrensrvcs/srp01.html.)

For a family program called Bookamania, we developed a scavenger hunt based on *The Wizard of Oz* Web sites, which will be used as an activity during the daylong program. September is our library card campaign month, and we support it by mounting a short page about the process (www.chipublib.org/008subject/003cya/campaign00.html).

We feature a short Internet safety quiz as well, which stays up year-round. We wrote the Internet safety quiz after looking at several examples, both on- and offline. There seemed to be common threads

Figures 1-5 and 1-6: Children are congratulated for choosing the correct answer to one of the questions featured on Chicago Public Library's Internet safety quiz game (www.chipublib.org/008subject/003cya/sign/safety2.html).

If I see stuff on the internet that makes me uncomfortable, should I keep it a secret?   YES   NO

That's Right. It isn't a good idea.

If you are at home, tell your parents right away if you come across any information that makes you feel uncomfortable.

If you are at the public library, tell a librarian and then leave that page right away.

NEXT

carried through all the examples: things like not providing identifying information, the importance of parental supervision, feeling safe while "cruising," not arranging to meet someone, and responding to inappropriate posts. After screening the examples, we wrote questions that would allow us to reiterate our policies in an engaging manner.

The look—which, as far as kids are concerned, is just as important as the information—was developed by Steve Jones from our computer services department. There are two people in that department who work with the Web. Neither one is really a Webmaster; we don't have anyone in a position like that. But Steve is our Web guru. After I do the basic HTML, he makes my files sing and dance.

The Sign of the Owl opening art was actually done a couple of years ago by James Wright, an artist who retired from our graphics department. He's done one for each season. The spring image is the result of the combined efforts of Jimmy; an artist Ross Karreman, in our graphics department, who contributed the gopher popping up; and Steve, who put it all together. I usually provide the content and basic text formatting.

Our process is fairly informal. When we decide to do something, I let Steve know in advance that it's coming. The text is developed in the children's and young adult services department and then sent to Steve with some idea of what we hope is possible (in terms of bells and whistles). I should say that Steve always manages to surprise us. He's wonderful.

For Bookamania, I'll develop a special page of links that will support a scavenger hunt about *The Wizard of Oz*. It will probably be a text file, so I'll write it, arrange it, and then see if Steve has graphics or some idea that will make it more interesting—some exciting way to make it "pop."

Insights & Improvements

We still need to split the site, creating a specific section for teens. This will increase our traffic and provide more useful, recreational, and educational information for older youth (ages 15 to 19.)

Contact Person

Cindy C. Welch, Young Adult Specialist
Children's and Young Adult Services
Chicago Public Library
400 South State Street, 10-S
Chicago, IL 60605
(312) 747-4780

COLLEGE INFORMATION ON THE WEB PROGRAM FOR YOUNG ADULTS

AKRON-SUMMIT COUNTY PUBLIC LIBRARY, NORTON BRANCH, OHIO

www.ascpl.lib.oh.us/br-ntn01.html

Overview

Recent surveys of Internet use among teenagers confirm what librarians have been observing for years. The Internet plays a vital role in the lives of many young adults, especially as a means for socializing with friends. The Pew Internet Project found that of the 17 million 12- to 17-year-olds who report using the Internet, 92 percent of them send and receive e-mail, and 74 percent of them have used instant messaging. Surfing the Web for fun, visiting entertainment sites, and playing games are also listed as the most popular teen activities online. But 66 percent of these teens also have used the Internet to research a product or service before buying it.

A college education could well be one of the most expensive products or services young adults (and/or their parents) purchase. Those with access to the Internet can now more easily investigate different college programs and their costs as an increasing number of colleges and universities market their educational programs via the Web. More and more colleges also are making their college admission applications available online.

Librarian Jan Chapman has been helping the young adults in her community plan and prepare for the future by conducting a program that demonstrates the different Web sites teens might use to research colleges and find information about financial aid options. At a time when many parents might not be aware of the information available on the Net or how to access it, a library program like this could make all the difference for young adults who are considering college but aren't sure where to go or how to get there.

At the end of the report, you'll find a list of the Web sites included on the "College Planning" handout that program participants receive. Some additional college planning Web sites are included in the Chapter Notes and References for this chapter.

Program Title

College Information on the World Wide Web

Target Audience

Senior high school students in grades 9 through 12, and interested parents
(Reported by Jan Chapman, young adult librarian)

Required Equipment

The program is held in the library's meeting room, which can accommodate up to 100 people. The program is designed for a maximum of 30 participants. A laptop computer with a connection to the Internet and an LCD computer projector are used to display each Internet site on the projector screen. A Web browser is required for displaying the Web sites. I used Internet Explorer.

Program Description

The purpose of the program is to acquaint high school students and their parents with the extensive and valuable information available on the World Wide Web to assist them with college planning. The program is designed to take each participant on a tour of selected college information Web sites.

At the beginning of the program, I give a brief talk on the importance of the Internet to colleges and mention how colleges are increasingly relying on their Web sites to attract prospective students. Each participant receives a handout that lists each Web site visited during the program, along with its URL, so they can continue exploring these resources at home or at the library.

I click on each Web site and briefly visit the various resources available on the site. The topics covered during the presentation include career exploration, student life at college, finding the right college using an online matchmaking service, financial aid and scholarships, scholastic aptitude tests (SAT, ACT), virtual tours of college campuses, online college applications, and tips on writing college admission essays.

As this is essentially a passive program, I ask participants to volunteer for the interactive aspects of some of the Web sites. For example, the Web site "Going to College" has a college matchmaker service that allows students to enter information in an interactive form and then be matched with colleges that fit their specifications. A selected participant gives me the requirements to complete the form, and I am able to show the colleges that meet his or her criteria.

I wrap up the program by showing the participants a Web site that gives information on national college fairs in their area. I refer them to a display table set up with a selection of college information books, such as the *Peterson's* and *Princeton Review* college guides. I also have on hand FAFSA (Free Application for Federal Student Aid) applications and brochures.

Insights & Improvements

I do feel it is important to mention to the participants that I am not a college or guidance counselor, nor a specialist in the college admissions process. My role as librarian is to point the way to valuable information on the World Wide Web. I also caution participants to be aware that some Web sites are more reliable in accuracy of content than others. However, the Internet is the wave of the future in the college admissions process, and students will need direction from information providers in choosing the best Web sites to assist them with planning.

Figure 1-7: Young adults can research college choices with the aid of Web sites selected by librarians at Akron-Summit County Public Library. The selected sites are distributed as bookmarks.

College Planning Web Sites

a listing of helpful Web sites compiled by the Akron-Summit County Public Library

Career/Major

Going to College—includes matchmaker service which helps you select a school based on your interests
http://www.embark.com/ugrad.asp

Mapping Your Future—a good general college information site
http://www.mapping-your-future.org

Princeton Review—advice on colleges/careers, with a yearly ranking of colleges by students
http://www.review.com/college/

College Planning Web Sites—A listing of helpful Web sites compiled by the Akron-Summit County Public Library

- Career/Major
  Going to College - includes matchmaker service which helps you select a school based on your interests.
  www.embark.com/college/ugrad_research.asp
  Mapping Your Future – a good general college information site
  www.mapping-your-future.org/

Princeton Review – advice on colleges/careers, with a yearly ranking of colleges by students.
www.review.com/college/index_no_login.cfm

- Testing
  ACT – register, test dates, test prep
  www.act.org/aap/regist/actdates.html
  SAT – register, test dates, sample questions, application process, financial aid
  www.collegeboard.com/

- Selecting a College
  My College Guide – answers to everyday questions about selecting a college, the application process, and financial aid.
  www.mycollegeguide.org/
  Ohio Board of Regents – college and university homepages
  www.regents.state.oh.us/visit_campuses.htm
  U.S. Two-Year Colleges – homepages
  http://cset.sp.utoledo.edu/twoyrcol.html
  Ohio Association of Community Colleges – homepages
  www.ohiocc.org/

- Campus Tours
  College and University Tour – virtual tours
  www.petersons.com/ugrad/
  Campus Tour – go on a virtual campus tour of your college campus
  www.campustours.com

- Admissions Process
  Peterson's Electronic Applications – apply to college online
  www.petersons.com/features/apply2.html
  CollegeView – comprehensive college information with great tips on writing the college admissions essay
  www.collegeview.com/
  100Hot/College – links to the top 100 college Web sites, ranked by number of hits.
  www.100hot.com/directory/education/college.html

- College Rankings
  US News and World Report College Rankings
  www.usnews.com/usnews/edu/college/cohome.htm
  College and University Rankings
  www.library.uiuc.edu/edx/rankings.htm

- Financial Aid
  FAFSA on the Web – apply online
  www.fafsa.ed.gov/
  The Smart Student Guide to Financial Aid – comprehensive collection of information about financial aid
  www.finaid.org/

Fast Web – free scholarship search
www.fastWeb.com/
- Additional College Planning Web Sites
  Fresch Free Scholarship Search – financial aid advice for the traditional and the non-traditional student
  www.freschinfo.com/index.phtml
  International Study and Travel Center – study programs, scholarships and work options
  www.istc.umn.edu/
  Wired Scholar – comprehensive college information including selecting a college, the campus visit, interviews, the admission process, and financial aid
  www.wiredscholar.com/paying/content/index.jsp

Contact Person

Jan Chapman, Intermediate/Young Adult Librarian
Akron-Summit County Public Library, Norton Branch
3930 South Cleve-Mass Road
Norton, OH 44203
(330) 825-7800
jchapman@ascpl.lib.oh.us

Chapter 2

Curriculum-Related Programs

In Linda Ellerbee's novel *Girl Reporter Blows Lid Off Town!* the main character, middle schooler Casey Smith, decided to investigate the possibility that the local paper mill was polluting the town's river. But Casey didn't go to the library to research paper manufacturing, she went home to her room and: "turned on the computer, began punching keys and started surfing the Net. . . . I found a page with a link to the mill's Web site. Clicking on the link, I watched as the page started to paint on the screen . . ." (p. 48). After reading about the history of the mill and its environmental report, Casey "tapped into the on-line encyclopedia to learn how a paper mill operates." She explains she "downloaded articles about the impact of paper manufacturing on the ecosystem . . . hit on a campaign for stronger government regulations of industry waste" and "searched environmental interest groups" (p. 50).

Searching for Internet sources that help illuminate a research question is just the kind of investigative activity many school media specialists might incorporate into a lesson. But the scene above perpetuates the myth that "everything is on the Net" and can be easily discovered just by punching keys and clicking. Librarians need to help students determine when the Internet might be the best source of information for their research and how to find useful Internet resources.

Online searching skills must be taught, just as students are taught how to use an encyclopedia, take notes, or write a grammatically correct sentence. Reports from educators indicate that students are not as savvy in their searching skills as they (or their teachers) might think. Martha Peet, Web researcher with the Texas Center for Educational Technology told *School Library Journal*, "Librarians assume kids know more than they really do about finding answers online" (Minkel, 2000: 22).

Just because children are using the Internet, clicking on links, and printing out pages, doesn't mean that they understand this medium or how best to search the millions of pages on the World Wide Web to find what interests them.

This chapter provides examples of the lessons, programs, and Web pages that school and public librarians have developed to teach children how to search for information on the Web, and which incorporate the use of the Web to present a research question and enhance the research process.

One of the Web-based activities that educators have developed to enhance student research experiences is known as a WebQuest. "A WebQuest is an inquiry-oriented activity in which most or all of the information used by learners is drawn from the Web. WebQuests are designed to use learners' time well, to focus on using information rather than looking for it, and to support learners' thinking at the levels of analysis, synthesis and evaluation. The model was developed in early 1995 at San Diego State University by Bernie Dodge with Tom March, and was outlined then in 'Some Thoughts About WebQuests'" (Dodge).

Librarian Debbie Abilock originated one of her impressive WebQuests while participating in the Library of Congress's American Fellows program. In this chapter she describes her guide to researching the *Turn-of-the-Century Child* program.

Other librarians have found it essential to devote some of their curriculum time to teaching students how to use Internet search tools. Despite the confident manner in which many elementary and secondary grade level students surf the Web, librarians are finding they do not truly understand Internet search tools. An article in the September 2000 *School Library Media Research* online journal notes: "Surprisingly little research has been conducted on children's Web searching behavior. Presumably this will change as Internet use spreads in schools nationwide. In contrast to the stereotype of today's children as computer-savvy Internet experts, the results of the few studies conducted to date found that middle and high school students have surprisingly low levels of success using the Web as a search tool" (Broch, 2000).

Alice Yucht, teacher-librarian at Heritage Middle School in New Jersey, agrees. "Students need to know how to actually search effectively and efficiently!! Many middle-schoolers think that Yahoo or AOLsearch will get them everything they need, because they don't really know much about online search tools and how to use them.

In the 'old days' we taught students the parts of the book, as an introduction to how information can be formatted and structured. Now we (librarians and teachers) need to teach kids:

1. How to choose and use the different kinds of search tools (e.g., directories, indexes, search engines, meta-searchers, and portals).
2. How to structure their search terminology (keywords, Boolean operators, etc.) to best effect. The kinds of higher-order thinking skills necessary to formulate an effective search query don't just happen; they have to be carefully—and developmentally— taught as integral information literacy skills.
3. How to evaluate what they find on the Web, since ANYONE can 'publish' there!"

Yucht's comments reflect my experiences as a children's librarian in a public library serving a large population of elementary and middle-school students who come to the library for homework assistance. In December 2000, an elementary grade level student was in the library looking for information on folic acid. He wanted more than the one or two sentences we were locating on folic acid in our science encyclopedias and books on nutrition. When I suggested we try to search for information on the Internet, he replied, "I've already been looking all over AOL and I haven't found anything." Before I could explain that America Online is not the Internet and convince him to try searching online with me, he left the department. Curious, I continued the search for folic acid to see what might be available on the Web.

Believing that this topic was not likely to have been indexed in any of the search tools designed for kids, I started with Google (www.google.com) and typed "folic acid" into the search window. The site at the top of the results list was a page called "Why Folic Acid Is So Important" from the Centers for Disease Control and Prevention. A couple of other sites on the results list, including the Vitamin and Mineral Guide from ThriveOnline, led to sources that provided suitable information for an elementary age child to add to his report and his understanding of this vitamin.

Many public libraries have traditionally dedicated library staff, services, and materials to help support the curriculum of their local schools. This tradition of service has evolved to include developing Web sites that list homework help resources, using the Web to solicit assignment alerts from teachers, and teaching students how to use Internet search tools. The report for Multnomah County Library describes what a public library can accomplish on a large scale, but its service goals can be adapted to smaller libraries as well.

The libraries that share information in this section about the various ways they are either teaching how to use Internet search tools available on the Web, or using the Web to support student research, include school libraries:

- Heritage Middle School, New Jersey
  Web page for Library Search Tools and Pathfinders
- Springfield Township High School, Pennsylvania
  WebQuest on Evaluating Web sites
- The Ellis School, Pennsylvania
  Lesson Plan for Learning to Use Search Tools
- The Nueva School, California
  Turn-of-the-Century Child Research Guide

And public libraries:

- Multnomah County Library, Oregon
  The School Corps Web site and program
- Monroe County Public Library, Indiana
  Web page for What Would You Like to Know about Indiana?

These provide just a sample of how teachers and school librarians across the country are using the Web in amazingly innovative ways with their students. The WebQuest and Educational Portal resource lists in Chapter 5 lead to additional examples of the variety of research projects and activities that incorporate student use of the Web. These resources and those found in the Search Tools list in Chapter 5 will provide you with further information to assist you in developing student online searching skills and helping children and young adults become smart users of Internet resources.

LIBRARY HOME PAGE FOR LIBRARY SEARCH TOOLS AND PATHFINDERS

HERITAGE MIDDLE SCHOOL LIBRARY, NEW JERSEY

www.members.home.net/hmslibrary/index.html

Overview

Teacher-Librarian Alice Yucht uses her library's homepage as a way to promote search tools she recommends students use for help with research assignments. A page she created called "Searching the Web" (www.members.home.net/hmslibrary/gosearch.html) features a list of suggested search tools. Another section called "Project Pathfinders" (www.members.home.net/hmslibrary/projects.html) outlines specific print and electronic resources and Web sites Yucht has identified as useful for the distinct topics students are researching.

Two of the hottest topics in education these days are inquiry-based learning and integrating technology into the classroom curriculum, states Yucht. "The first is certainly nothing new to librarians; we've been helping kids with research projects for years, and many of us are already the techno-leaders in our schools, either by choice or by default.

"Many of our students run to the Web for research of any kind, even though they haven't yet learned strategic search skills. Many of our teachers now want their students to use resources beyond the textbook, classroom, and even the school building itself, but are nervous about what might be found out there."

The banner on Heritage Middle School Library's Web page says: "It's an information jungle out there—let a librarian be your guide!" Project Pathfinder and portal pages are a very successful way to demonstrate to both in-school and outside communities how and why a professional information guide is a primary resource for every school.

Program Title

Pathfinders for Class Projects
www.members.home.net/hmslibrary/projects.html

Target Audience

Middle school students
(*Reported by Alice Yucht, school media specialist for Heritage Middle School Library in New Jersey*)

Required Equipment

Computer with access to the Internet and a Web browser

Program Description

I first developed the "Searching the Web" search tools page as a way to get the kids beyond Yahoo! and AOL search. I also wanted to make sure that the students would have easy access to other search tools, whether they were in the library, in the computer lab, or at home.

Figures 2-1 and 2-2: The homepage for the Heritage Middle School Library includes links to Project Pathfinders, search tools, and other helpful student resources (http://members.home.net/hmslibrary/index.html).

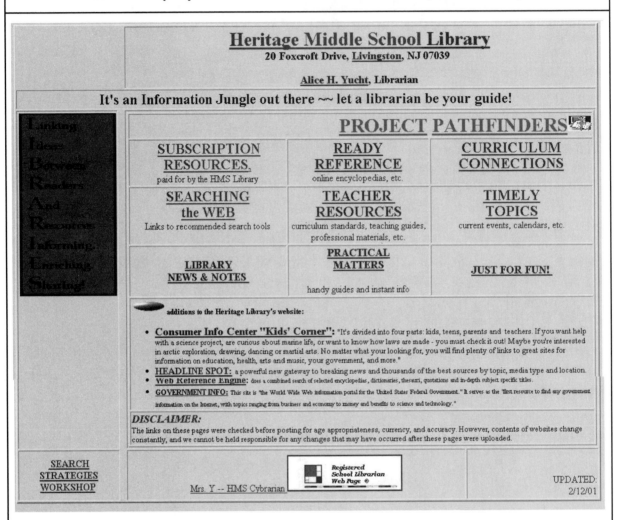

(The original, barebones version of this page was actually the beginning of the library's Web site. Using the search page as a homepage, I could teach the students about the different search tools and still bring them back to "home" when needed.)

When it comes to using the Web, kids think they know more than they do, but they are also willing to learn because they don't think using the Web is work. They aren't afraid to click on anything; in fact, that's half the fun—to see where you might end up. But they need a structured learning environment if they're going to be kept on task.

Teachers need to understand that they can't just tell kids to "go find . . . ." There's too much stuff out there that's worthless. Both students and teachers need basic lessons in media literacy and how to evaluate what's out there. Librarians are the most likely people to be teaching these skills, but we've got to convince the teachers that this must be an integral component of today's education.

The Project Pathfinders I develop—one-page guides to appropriate resources for inquiry-based activities—are an effective way to demonstrate the value of teacher-librarian collaboration for successful student learning. These guides steer students toward the most useful resources both within and beyond the library walls, help develop effective research skills, ensure that they *will* find the information they need to complete the project, and even help keep students on task as they explore.

During January and February 2001, the Project Pathfinders page provided guides for a sixth grade class studying black history; a seventh grade civics class researching executive agencies; an eighth grade world history class studying Africa, Asia, and the Americas; an eighth grade family science class researching careers; a gifted/talented/enrichment class researching various interest clusters on the stock market, forensics, inventions, and more; and a music class studying various composers.

Project Pathfinders can be either paper handouts or portal pages on a library Web site, as long as they include (at the minimum):

- Recommended keywords and search terms to use
- Dewey numbers and/or useful print materials
- URLs or hot links to age-appropriate sites online, and any necessary instructions for accessing information in those sites
- Citation formats to document the resources used.

Once you've got the template set up, constructing a Pathfinder for a specific unit can take anywhere from an hour to a full day, depending on the scope of the assignment and the variety and accessibility of the resources to be included.

I start with a list of relevant subject headings and search terms, and always ask the teacher for any additional keywords that have been emphasized in the classroom curriculum. Next are the library materials, listing reference sources and Dewey numbers for the topics to be investigated, but rarely specifying individual titles.

Finding and deciding which URLs to include on Pathfinder pages should be just another part of our ongoing collection development responsibilities. Just as we read reviews and examine new titles for possible purchase of print resources, we need to keep track of recommended Web sites for curriculum consideration.

Among the many sources I use for URLs of Web sites to consider are *Web Feet*, a print subscription, published by RockHill Press,

Classroom Connect's best of the Web resources (www.classroom.com/ library/cybrariansCorner.jhtml), Kathy Schrock's *Guide for Educators* (www.discoveryschool.com/schrockguide/), *Digital Librarian* (www.digital-librarian.com/), *Kids Report* (www.madison.k12.wi.us/ tnl/detectives/), and, of course, recommendations from other school librarians on LM_Net, the electronic listserv for school media specialists.

I used to keep an ongoing database file on my hard drive so that I could add possibilities whenever I found them. Now, however, I save them to my Backflip account (www.backflip.com), a free Web site service that organizes my saved sites into broad subject-area folders, accessible from any connected computer station. This way, I don't have to worry about losing my consideration file, and teachers can also add URLs for their subject areas.

Although I used to give out printed Pathfinders when the class came to the library, I now only post them on the library's Web site, and use the page as the starting point for each class library activity. These online guides serve as effective portal pages for the students' research (efficiently demonstrating how to integrate info-tech into the curriculum) and as excellent public relations devices for the library's programs and services, for the following reasons:

- Teachers must collaborate with me for a Pathfinder Page to be developed for their class or subject. Because I've done the preliminary searching, sorting, and sifting, teachers know that their students will be able to find the information they need quickly and efficiently, without wasting time in useless or inappropriate sites. The teacher who does not choose to use the library *and* the librarian, however, does not get this service.
- Parents can check the library Web page to find out what research projects are currently in progress and what resources are being recommended for use. The student who says, "I couldn't get to the library" no longer has an excuse, since the library is now coming to the student.
- Because the Pathfinder Pages are now accessible from both school and home, there is no need to copy down URLs from the blackboard or another screen, or to bookmark URLs on different machines.
- When the class comes to the library, I use the Pathfinder to explain and review the use of both print and online resources, and teach any specific research skills needed for a project.
- With a limited number of Net access stations in the library, I insist that students use the links from the Pathfinder Pages before I will allow use of any other general search engines. This ensures that time online in the library is used wisely, productively, and equitably.

- On every Pathfinder Page I include a link to Noodlebibs (www.noodletools.com/noodlebib/), a free Web-based service that simplifies the process of creating and editing MLA-style bibliographies, once basic bibliographic information is provided. Students are required to do a bibliography for each project, and this helps them document their resources as they are using them.
- Specific Pathfinder Pages are available online only for the duration of that project. I upload or remove pages as necessary to keep them current. Whenever a new or useful Web site is found for a project, I can update that Pathfinder Page and have the information available to everyone immediately.

Insights & Improvements

This is a never-ending job! I keep a hard copy of every Pathfinder and resource page in a binder. As I add new resources to the collection, I pencil them onto the paper copy so that I can add them to the Web page when I update it. I also remove Pathfinders from the Web site when the project is finished. This keeps everything fairly current, and also means that I have some control over who uses those pathfinders and how they are being used beyond my immediate school community.

Pathfinders are a very valuable form of public relations for the library. Because I only create Pathfinders when the teachers actually collaborate with me on projects, more and more teachers are using the library and consulting with me before they give the assignment to the kids. I also put notices in the monthly parent newsletter about new Pathfinders currently available. This is also a nifty way to let parents know that "the library is closed" is no longer a viable excuse for kids.

It's important to include both print and online resources. Kids need to know (and be reminded) that good old books are still useful and valuable resources. In my library we *always* start with the print resources, in order to have a better idea of what we're looking for (and which keywords are most likely to be useful). And Web connections have been known to fail, so you've got to have other sources available!

Putting up a Pathfinder saves you time, paper, and aggravation in the long run.

Contact Person

Alice Yucht, Teacher-Librarian
Heritage Middle School

20 Foxcroft Drive
Livingston, NJ 07039
aliceinfo@excite.com

WEBQUEST ON EVALUATING WEB SITES

SPRINGFIELD TOWNSHIP HIGH SCHOOL LIBRARY, PENNSYLVANIA

http://mciunix.mciu.k12.pa.us/~spjvWeb/

Overview

Via the Internet, Librarian Joyce Kasman Valenza shares a wealth of information with both her students and her peers about using the Web to access information. Valenza writes a weekly column for the *Philadelphia Enquirer*, regularly contributes articles to various professional publications, and conducts workshops about technology in education. She saves much of her work to her personal homepage, www.joycevalenza.com/.

The homepage for her library also serves as an inviting gateway to the tools and strategies for developing information literacy. In fact, it exemplifies just what she advises the purpose of a library's homepage should be:

"Your library Web page is your second front door. It creates signage for students and staff. The effective library Web page pulls together, in one unified interface, all of a library's resources—print and electronic. It offers guidance while it fosters independent learning. It models careful selection. It offers valuable public service and can redefine 'community.' It can even lead users back to print. A good library Web page offers implicit instruction and projects an important image of the librarian as an information professional" (Valenza, 2000).

In addition to the professional guidance she offers through the library's Web site, Valenza provides personal instruction to her students to help increase their understanding of Internet search tools and how best to use them to find answers to their research questions. Her guided outlines for teaching students about Internet search tools and how to evaluate Web sites also include complementary pages for the teachers of the lessons, explaining how they fit with

Figure 2-3: More helpful links for students and teachers appear below this image map on the homepage for the Springfield Township High School Virtual Library (http://mciunix.mciu.k12.pa.us/~spjvweb/).

Springfield Township High School
Virtual Library

General info

Our Mission

Our Staff

MLA style sheet

Email

Our District

Links for Students

Policies

Librarian Stuff

SEARCH HERE!

Links for Teachers

College and Career

© Art by Emily Valenza

Reference Desk

NEW!

Catalogs and databases

Mrs. V's Homepage

curriculum standards, what resources are needed, and other tips for implementing the lesson. These additional instructional guides are available at SearchQuest: Teacher Page (http://mciunix.mciu.k12.pa.us/~spjvweb/sqteach.html) and Evaluating Web Sites: Teacher Page (http://mciu.org/~spjvweb/evalwebteach.html).

Program Title

SearchQuest: A WebQuest About Search Tools
http://mciu.org/~spjvweb/sqstu.html

Target Audience

This activity has been used successfully with ninth grade communications arts students, with graduate students, and in professional development workshops with teachers and librarians.
(*Reported by Joyce Valenza, library information specialist for Springfield Township High School, Pennsylvania*)

Required Equipment

Computer with Web connection and projection system. I usually run this in a computer lab with at least one computer per small group of three or four. Sometimes I have asked students to develop a poster or brochure for their search tool. This works nicely using Microsoft Publisher.

Program Description

Although my students are Web-confident, most have very limited searching tool kits. Many depend on Yahoo! or Excite or AOL. These are curable conditions. I wanted them to see the broad searching world beyond the one URL they remembered. Many of us use only one or two search tools, but the landscape is constantly changing and there are many worthy new and underused tools to try.

The outline for the SearchQuest project explains that each group of students will become expert in one search tool and demonstrate it by creating a commercial, "selling" its best features to the class.

> As you examine the search tool, record any relevant information in your organizer. You may wish to divide your group into specialties to cover ground more efficiently (result list, search tips, special services). Please use the glossary if you are unfamiliar with any terms.

1. Visit the search tool site and carefully examine the features on its front page.
2. Determine what type of search tool you are working with. Is it a subject directory, search engine or meta-search engine?
3. Visit the help or tips page. What are the "secrets" of the search tool?
4. Carefully examine and evaluate the search tool so that you know its best and worst features.
5. Is there a place for expert searchers? What special features does it offer?
6. Are there any other special features, such as image searching, translation, or subject trees?
7. How are results organized and displayed? Are there summaries? Annotations? Keywords?
8. Are the first two or three pages of results highly relevant?
9. Try at least two searches to "road test" your search tool.

General topic: movie reviews.

A complicated search with more than one concept. For example, find a recipe for chocolate chip cookies (sample strategy: +recipe +"chocolate chip cookies").

1. Use your organizer to help you design a two-minute commercial to sell your search tool to the group. Decide how you will present. Remember to use advertising language and to include those slightly negative features consumers need to know, as "small print" at the end of your presentation.
2. Present your commercial to the group. You must demonstrate the features by giving the class an actual tour of the tool's features.
3. Following the presentations, the class will rank and decide on awards for the search tools using the Award Organizer.

This activity is one strategy I have found to introduce and discuss a variety of search options with students. It is important to define terms such as a *subject directory* and *field searching* in advance, and to circulate while the groups are working, guiding students into discovering the best features of the various tools. Those features might not be immediately obvious to students who have not paid a great deal of attention to how search tools actually work.

Creating these commercials works because, after all, these tools are products. They are in competition with each other for the attention of information consumers. Following all the presentations, the class reaches consensus, ranking the search tools and awarding them specific honors, or Searchie Awards. Scaffolding [tip sheets and other instructional aids] is provided to guide students as they examine their search tools.

Before this activity, I update the search tool list and make sure I am aware of the new tricks some of the old search tools have added. I always learn something new from my students' presentations.

Insights & Improvements

It is amazing how the activity works. The students complain at first: "But we already know how to search, Mrs. V!" After the activity I see them using tools they never used before, offering each other advice on which is the best choice for a particular job.

One of our teachers asks students to prepare a poster about a search tool they were not responsible for presenting. This not only ensures students listen during all presentations, but provides visual reinforcement in her classroom well after we've finished the activity.

Contact Person

Joyce Kasman Valenza, Librarian
Springfield Township High School Library

1801 East Paper Mill Road
Erdenheim, PA 19038
(215) 233-6058
joyce.valenza@phillynews.com

LESSON PLAN FOR LEARNING TO USE SEARCH TOOLS

THE ELLIS SCHOOL, PENNSYLVANIA

www.theellisschool.org/

Overview

At The Ellis School, a K-12 college preparatory school for women, Librarian Kathy Koenig teaches her students, starting in fifth grade, how to evaluate Web sites. But she waits until eighth grade to teach them Web searching skills. "There's a certain level of sophistication required for understanding some of the search concepts that may not be there at younger ages," she explains. "In eighth grade, students at Ellis are involved in a laptop immersion program, and I'm working with them a lot on search engines, databases, and advanced searching. I'm interested in using the Internet to teach critical thinking."

Although her lesson on Internet search engines requires the students to use various search tools to find different types of information, Koenig's lesson is not posted to the Web. Instead, students access the outline for the class by opening a folder on the network. This folder contains the outline, with hot links to the search tools they are to use. Because each student has her own computer, she can type the answers on the outline sheet and save it with a separate filename for the teacher to review.

Program Title

There is no formal title; the program is integrated into the curriculum at all levels. The informal title, purloined from a summer workshop at Pitt, is *Filling in the Potholes on the Information Superhighway*.

Target Audience

Grade 8
(*Reported by Kathy Koenig, director of libraries for the Ellis School, Pennsylvania*)

Required Equipment

Network server, iBooks (other laptop or personal computers would work too) with Internet access and a Web browser

Program Description

Each eighth grader (38 in the 2000-2001 school year) has her own school-owned iBook. This lesson could easily be done with fewer students in a lab if kids worked together. We don't use a computer projector. One could be used if students didn't have access to their own computers, but the practice exercises would be harder to do.

We used Appleworks 6 software, but anything that supports hot links will work. (We happen to be a mostly Mac platform institution, as many schools are.)

The course outline is saved on the network server in a "GetBox" or teacher folder. We tell students at the beginning of class what the file is named and they can open it. We did it that way so that the students could write on the document when completing the search exercises and put it into the "DropBox" folder on the network where I could pick it up and check it. They wouldn't have been able to do that on a Web page.

With the laptop immersion program, it was expected that a large portion of research would be done on the Internet. Past experience has demonstrated thoroughly that the girls are terrible at searching. The goal is to make them more efficient and effective searchers; ultimately, to provide them with skills they will need at all levels and in all classes. (And to make my own job easier by not having to teach these search techniques 20 times a year!)

I prepared two lessons: the first on search engines (what they are, how they are different, how to find them) and the second on advanced search techniques (Boolean operators, nesting, truncation/wildcard, and so on). In the first lesson, URL addresses of relevant search engines are hot linked so that the girls can go right to them to see what I am talking about. I also added a search engine guide for future reference and practice exercises.

The basic outline for the course is as follows:

Search Engines
　Search Engine: a program that links indexed pages
　　Yahoo—www.yahoo.com
　　Excite— www.excite.com
　　HotBot—www.hotbot.com
　Metasearch engine: A search engine that searches many search engines
　　Metacrawler—www.metacrawler.com/index.html
　　IXQuick—www.ixquick.com
　　FastSearch—www.ussc.alltheweb.com
　Portals: subject-specific search engines
　　Medical Matrix—www.medmatric.org/reg/login.asp
　　SciSeek—www.sciseek.com
　　FindLaw—www.findlaw.com
　Subject Directories: resources selected and classified into categories by humans
　　About.com—www.about.com
　　Argus—www.clearinghouse.net
　　Internet Public Library—www.ipl.org

Things You Need to Understand about Search Engines

1. No search engine indexes everything.
2. Not every search engine indexes the same pages.
3. Advanced searching techniques will not be the same on every search engine.

Evaluating Search Engines
　Relevance
　Size of database
　Design/accessibility (ease of use and navigation)
　How current is it?
　Stability

1. Find the URL address for each of the following organizations:
   * National Gallery of Art
   * NASA
   * Library of Congress
   * Which search engines did you use?
   * Which gave the best results? Why?
2. Find information about the Harry Potter movie.
   * What is the URL of the best site?
   * Which search engines did you use?
   * Which gave the best results? Why?

3. Find some research-quality resources about endangered species from either government or nonprofit sources.
   - List at least three sites.
   - Which search engines did you use?
   - Which gave the best results? Why?

The second lesson, Advanced Search Techniques, concentrates on the actual construction of a search. This lesson discusses what to do when a weak search yields poor results, for example, too many hits, not enough hits, inaccurate or irrelevant hits. After I remind students that each search tool employs different advanced searching protocols, they learn various methods for refining or expanding a search by using truncation or wild cards, limiters, Boolean operators, and nesting terms. Students then practice what they have learned by using advanced search techniques to find, for example, a recipe for Norwegian Christmas cookies called "krumkake," or the name of the first American woman to win a gold medal for figure skating in the Olympics. They are asked such questions as: How did you construct your search? If you didn't find what you wanted the first time, how did you refine the search? What was the successful search?

Because there are so many ways to get results, often the "best" answer isn't a given, or even obvious. I generally have several groups work on the same question, then we discuss the strategy each used and make comparisons of things like result lists, accuracy of information found, ease of navigation, and so on.

Insights & Improvements

Test the sample search questions in advance. I'm a pretty avid advocate of free speech, but we do need to be careful about accessing "inappropriate" sites because we don't filter. Also, I like to make sure there really is information out there! Web searching is frustrating enough in reality without making it so in a lesson. I hope that finding things in a guided lesson will give them the confidence to keep going when they're on their own and they encounter difficulties.

Contact Person

Kathy Koenig, Director of Libraries
The Ellis School
6425 Fifth Avenue
Pittsburgh, PA 15206
(412) 661-5992
koenigk@theellisschool.org

TURN-OF-THE-CENTURY CHILD RESEARCH GUIDE

THE NUEVA SCHOOL, CALIFORNIA

www.nuevaschool.org/~debbie/library/overview.html

Overview

Librarian Debbie Abilock serves elementary and middle-level students at The Nueva School in California, a progressive school for gifted and talented children emphasizing integrated studies, creative arts, and social-emotional learning. As the curriculum, library, and technology coordinator for Nueva, Abilock has been utilizing the Web to teach critical thinking and develop her students' information literacy skills, and to share what she knows with her colleagues around the world. Public, K-12, and university libraries have linked to "Choose the Best Search for Your Information Needs," a table she created to help students determine the best search engine to use for their research (www.nuevaschool.org/~debbie/library/research/adviceengine.html).

Some of Abilock's most innovative work appears in the Web-based research projects she has developed for her students. The detailed Web guides (what many refer to as WebQuests) she creates in collaboration with Nueva School teachers lead students through an array of sources they might consider when investigating an issue or answering a complex question. While the world was still waiting to learn whether George Bush or Al Gore would become America's 43rd president in November 2000, Abilock was developing a research structure to help students examine "The Presidential Election 2000: Who Holds the Power?" (www.nuevaschool.org/~debbie/library/cur/hum/power.html).

Abilock, who also serves as editor of *Knowledge Quest*, the journal for the American Association of School Librarians, reports below on a project she developed in 1999 while participating in the Library of Congress's American Fellows Program, a program for outstanding humanities teachers and media specialists to learn about American Memory primary sources and their use in the classroom.

Figure 2-4: Students can click on the stars to view photographs of children from the turn of the 20th century before beginning to investigate their history.

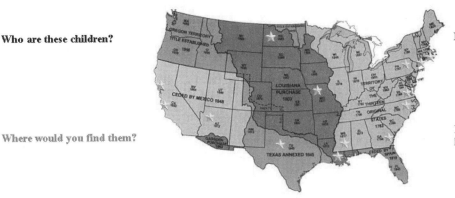

TNEVA Library/Humanities/Computer Curriculum

Turn-of-the-Century Child

Who are these children?

Examine their faces...

Where would you find them?

How are they like you?

Enter the world of the turn-of-the-century child... ▶▶

Admission of States and Territorial Acquistion (modified)
U.S. Bureau of the Census. "Historical Maps of the United
States," from The Perry-Castañeda Library Map Collection,
The University of Texas at Austin
[http://www.lib.utexas.edu/Libs/PCL/Map_collection/histus.html]

Program Title

Turn-of-the-Century Child
www.NuevaSchool.org/~debbie/library/cur/20c/turn.html

Target Audience

Middle school (although this project can be adapted up to the high school level and down to younger students, depending on what you require them to do)
(*Reported by Debbie Abilock, curriculum, library and technology co-ordinator, The Nueva School, California*)

Required Equipment

Computers with Web browsers and access to the Internet, a scanner, and your school library. We used Netscape Composer for making Web pages. You can use much more sophisticated authoring software.

If you want to include on the Web copies of documents the kids create, such as their diary entries, you'll want to create Adobe Acrobat versions, which can be done right in Microsoft Word, or you can scan in pictures and other images.

We worked both in the classroom and in the school library, which has the required equipment. Students should pair on computers for some of the activities, but each will create an individual "persona," so they need time on the computer individually. We didn't use a computer projector, but it might be useful depending on your working style and how many students you have.

Program Description

A humanities teacher and I were interested in learning how to use primary sources to engage students in history. Our own learning odyssey began as American Memory Scholars. We worked for a week with other educators and Library of Congress staff (historians and educators) to learn how to think about the way history is reconstructed from past evidence.

While we were encouraged by these wise people to think about creating a single lesson, over the course of the summer an idea emerged to develop an entire curriculum that immersed students in the rich period of 1900-1923, drawing parallels to 2000 as the new millennium emerged.

The first series of exercises, using primary source photographs of young children of diverse backgrounds, is designed to teach and practice the skills of observation and deduction to build student understanding of 1900-1923, the "first generation" of the 20th century. From the initial stimulus, a digitized photograph taken during the period, students develop a richly realized "persona" from the same geographic region and ethnic background as the child pictured.

Much as a historian fits a particular artifact into an assemblage of evidence for the purpose of constructing a model of the past, students identify, place, and interpret these images as part of their scrapbooks of an imagined child born in 1900.

In a parallel series of exercises students examine their own family's personal photographs in order to reinforce visual literacy skills, experience the process of historical inquiry, and recognize that their own lives are part of the historical record. The goal is a full understanding of how knowledge of the past is constructed from evidence interpreted by historians.

Our goal is to put students in the role of historians who engage in a genuine historical inquiry. Students act as if they are practicing professionals and incorporate a genuine information problem-solving process (library research) into all aspects of their project. As part of the development of historical thinking, they formulate questions, research the historical record, and consider multiple perspectives and judgments. Beyond a working knowledge of the events, ideas, and persons of the century, students construct an understanding of the major "themes" of the period and how these might impact a child born in 1900.

Based on their analyses, they assemble both a physical and digital album of letters, oral histories, artifacts, diary entries, narratives, and images based on an invented child within a family. From their investigations, students learn to describe the past through the eyes of those who were there, and create hypothetical, historically plausible narratives for their individual characters.

At Nueva, a curriculum like this is created in groups or teams. As a school librarian with goals of reading and research, the opportunity to be involved in an entire project allows me to design, deliver, and assess the curriculum collaboratively with a teacher. The sense of personal and professional satisfaction and the engagement with a group of children over time make such a venture so attractive, so much downright fun!

Author's note: The outline for the program is so richly layered and integrated with links to primary sources available on the Web that it is difficult to describe. It is something that must be seen and explored in order to fully appreciate the depth of the structure and the clear pathways that have been defined for finding ways to thoroughly investigate life in the 1900s.

There are many resources available for teachers and librarians interested in learning how to create their own Web-based pathfinder or WebQuest. In *Some Thoughts About WebQuests*, Dodge explains: "The first stage for a teacher in learning to be a WebQuest designer is to become familiar with the resources available on-line in their own content area" (1997).

This stage began for Abilock while learning about the Library of Congress's American Memory collection. Photographs from this collection comprise the "initial stimulus" for the inquiry process and prompt the questions posed on the homepage for *Turn-of-the-Century Child:* Who are these children? Where would you find them? How are they like you? The students' role as historians begins with the direction "examine their faces."

Abilock says that selecting the 14 stimuli photographs depicting children from the 1900s was both difficult and easy. "Generally it's hard to search by date, and you can't specify that you want to get pictures of children who were *born* in 1900. Again, for some parts of the country it was a snap! We could find multiple images from the Midwest and of children as oyster shuckers in Louisiana, but *try* to get something decent for California . . . or for Indians. This in itself becomes a discussion with the kids, because it means that the historical record is full of HOLES!'"

There was no need to scan any of the images that appear in *Turn-of-the-Century Child* pages. The images featured were found on the Web in the American Memory collection and inserted in the guide as saved images in .gif or .jpg format.

According to Dodge, the next step in developing a WebQuest is "to organize one's knowledge of what's out there. . . . Following that, teachers should identify topics that fit in with their curriculum and for which there are appropriate materials on-line." Abilock has several pages that serve to organize her knowledge of resources available to students for analyzing the historical record of life in the 1900s.

When students begin gathering materials to create a scrapbook depicting the life of their turn-of-the-century child, they can start their investigation with resources Abilock has collected on a page called "Creating a Child Born in 1900" (www.nuevaschool.org/~debbie/library/cur/20c/turn/sup/faq.html). This page is divided into sections listing resources for learning about what people did for fun, home life school and work, and more.

Students can also find resources by following the series of pages Abilock created to guide development of the scrapbook beginning with the turn-of-the-century child's birth (www.nuevaschool.org/~debbie/library/cur/20c/turn/scrapbk/birth.html). Two of the links on this first page in the "Begin a Scrapbook" series of pages lead to an index of genealogy sites for researching names and another page Abilock created explaining how to collect maps, pictures, photos, and prints for the project.

Abilock's Web guide for researching the turn-of-the-century child also includes detailed outlines for teachers. She provides an overview of the project, listing the stated objectives, time required, and resources used (www.nuevaschool.org/~debbie/library/cur/20c/turn/teach/lpover.html), as well as a detailed lesson plan describing the materials and procedures required for implementing the project and the basis for evaluating students' work (www.nuevaschool.org/~debbie/library/cur/20c/turn/teach/lp1.html).

Insights & Improvements

What's nice to know is that the project can be extended or limited based on the amount of time you want to devote to it. You can do one lesson to teach visual literacy, or spend an entire semester immersing students in the period. It can be modified by what you have available in print in your library, how much time and how many computers you have, and your technology expertise.

The American Memory collections (and now other digital library resources) are so rich in materials for this period that you have the opportunity to do the entire project online if you choose. On the other hand, if a technology "product" is not one of your goals, the students could create their scrapbooks as print products using images and words from these digital sites.

Contact Person

Debbie Abilock, Curriculum, Library, Technology Coordinator
The Nueva School
6565 Skyline Boulevard
Hillsborough, CA 94010
(650) 358-2272, ext. 5
debbie@nuevaschool.org
www.nuevaschool.org

THE SCHOOL CORPS WEB SITE AND PROGRAM

MULTNOMAH COUNTY LIBRARY, OREGON

www.multnomah.lib.or.us/

Overview

Some public libraries have been leaders in categorizing Web resources to help students locate information on the Internet that can answer homework questions and enhance research assignments. Libraries across the country link to Multnomah County Library's Homework Help page, an Internet subject directory consisting of Web sites and Web pages that specifically concentrate on homework-related

Figure 2-5: Multnomah County Library's School Corps Web site directs students, parents, teachers, and media specialists to useful online resources.

 Multnomah County Library   School Corps

The Multnomah County Library School Corps connects students and teachers with the critical information resources of the public library. The goal of the School Corps is to increase the information literacy of students in Multnomah County by working in partnership with local schools. Read more about the School Corps. **Note: School Corps services are available only to the students, teachers, and media specialists of Multnomah County.**

For Teachers and Media Specialists

- Educator Evening: Special training for teachers & media specialists.
- School Corps Menu of Services: All **free of charge**. Schedule training sessions for teachers or students.
- Assignment Alert: Take the time to tell us about your upcoming assignments and we'll make it worth your while with age-appropriate Web sites, booklists, and guides to research.
- CascadeLink Education Resources: Links to educational sites at all levels from K-12 to postsecondary.

For Students

- KidsPage for kids to 8th grade
- Homework Center for 3rd-12th grade
- Outernet for young adults (middle & high school)

For Parents

- Family Guide to the Web
- Helping Your Child With Homework

For more information or to book School Corps services, contact Jackie Partch, School Corps Team Leader, at 503.988.6004 or jacquelp@multcolib.org.
The address of this page is http://www.multcolib.org/schoolcorps/
This page was last updated Thursday, April 12, 2001.

subjects for grades K through 12. Although developed specifically to support the educational use of students and teachers in Multnomah County, Orgeon, the selection is valued by librarians across the country because every Web resource included on the comprehensive listing is reviewed by librarians from Multnomah County Library.

Multnomah County librarians also have been leaders in teaching their patrons about new electronic resources available at the library

Figure 2-6: Multnomah County Library's KidsPage! is regularly updated with current-event information.

and on the Internet. Since 1999, the Multnomah County School Corps librarians have hosted Web Camp, weeklong day camps for children ages 11 to 14 who work in groups to write and illustrate electronic magazines, put them on the Internet, and participate in other library-planned activities.

The following report describes the instructional Web pages and services that School Corps librarians provide to students during the school year.

Figure 2-7: Multnomah's carefully constructed directory of topical homework Web sites is used by libraries across the country.

Multnomah County Library   *Homework Center*

School Corps | Library Catalog | Library Databases | Para padres y maestros | Ask Us! Online

State Poetry Contest for Students

Homework Topics:

African-American Sites	General Reference	Native American Sites
American History	Geography	News & Current Events
Ancient & Classical Cultures	Government & Politics	Personal Finance
Animals	Health & Nutrition	Regional Information
The Arts	History	Religion
Astronomy & Space	Holidays & Celebrations	Science
Biographies	Language Arts	Social Issues
Biology	Literature & Authors	Sports
Computers & Inventions	Maps	States Information
Costumes & Clothing	Mathematics	Transportation
Countries & Flags	Music	Wars & World History
European History	Mysterious & Unexplained	What is a Search Engine?
Evaluating Web Sites	Mythology	What Makes a Community?

Program Title

Multnomah County Library School Corps
www.multnomah.lib.or.us/lib/schoolcorps

Target Audience

Students in grades 4 through 12 and school faculty for School Corps technology trainings, students in pre-K through grade 12 for the library's Web sites for kids and young adults
(Reported by Jackie Partch, School Corps team leader, Multnomah County Library)

Figure 2-8: Resources of particular interest to young adults are featured on Multnomah's Outernet.

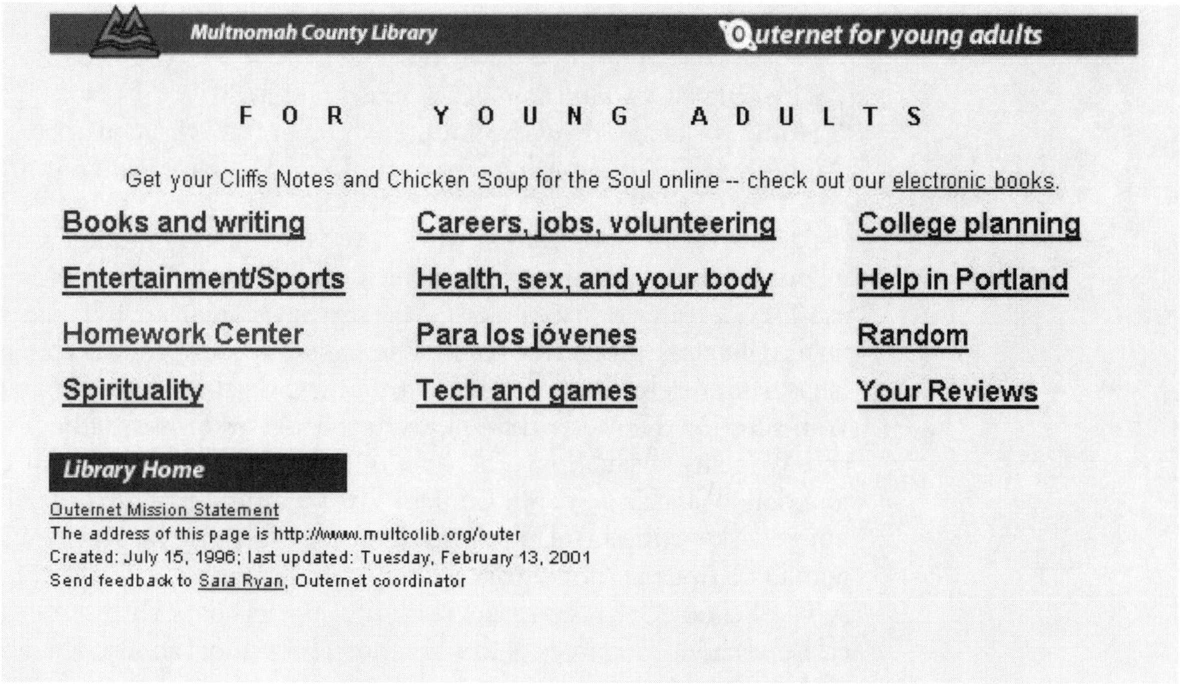

Multnomah County Library   Outernet for young adults

F O R   Y O U N G   A D U L T S

Get your Cliffs Notes and Chicken Soup for the Soul online -- check out our <u>electronic books</u>.

<u>Books and writing</u>   <u>Careers, jobs, volunteering</u>   <u>College planning</u>

<u>Entertainment/Sports</u>   <u>Health, sex, and your body</u>   <u>Help in Portland</u>

<u>Homework Center</u>   <u>Para los jóvenes</u>   <u>Random</u>

<u>Spirituality</u>   <u>Tech and games</u>   <u>Your Reviews</u>

Library Home

<u>Outernet Mission Statement</u>
The address of this page is http://www.multcolib.org/outer
Created: July 15, 1996; last updated: Tuesday, February 13, 2001
Send feedback to <u>Sara Ryan</u>, Outernet coordinator

Required Equipment

Because School Corps is an outreach program, we teach these classes in public and private schools throughout Multnomah County. We have also taught the classes a few times at branch libraries, but because of space considerations, we have found that it is often easier to teach the classes at schools. There was also less interest in classes offered at the library.

The classes can be taught in a classroom, library, or computer lab. For a demonstration, one computer is sufficient. However, students seem to understand better when they are able to use the products themselves, so a computer lab (or a library or classroom with multiple computers) is ideal. A projector is necessary if just one computer is used to do a demonstration. Although it is not necessary in a lab situation, it is much easier for the students to follow along if a projector is used. Internet access and a Web browser are required. School Corps librarians also use Microsoft PowerPoint for some presentations.

Program Description

Multnomah County Library has developed three Web sites for children and young adults to help children and young adults find information on the Internet:

KidsPage (www.multnomah.lib.or.us/lib/kids/)
Homework Center (www.multnomah.lib.or.us/lib/homework/)
Outernet for Young Adults (www.multnomah.lib.or.us/lib/outer/)

Part of the School Corps' work involves teaching students and school faculty about using these sites. We also teach about how to use DYNA (our library catalog), Magazines Online (our full-text articles database), and other library databases. Because we use the databases themselves to teach these trainings, we don't have separate Web sites for them. In addition, we teach classes on search engines and Web site evaluation. The handouts for these trainings can be found at "What Is a Search Engine?" (www.multnomah.lib.or.us/lib/homework/search.html) and "Evaluating Web Sites" (www.multnomah.lib.or.us/lib/homework/webeval.html).

The School Corps connects students and teachers with the critical information resources of the Multnomah County Library. The goal of the School Corps is to increase the information literacy of students in Multnomah County by working in partnership with local schools.

We have a prepared curriculum for each of the trainings we do, but we customize the instruction itself to make it more relevant to the students. School media specialists or teachers call me, the team leader, to schedule a date for us to come to the school to determine what type of resource (library catalog, magazine database, Web sites, or all of the above) the students need to learn about. I ask what the class will be studying at that time, so we can use those topics as examples in our presentation.

On the day of the training, one of our team members visits the school, sometimes taking along a laptop computer or computer projector if necessary (some schools already have the equipment we need). The team member sets up the equipment in the classroom, lab, or library, using the school's network connection or phone line to connect to the Internet. During the presentation itself, we talk about how to use the resource, using the topic(s) the class is studying as an example in our searches.

Depending on the age of the students, we might distribute informational sheets, fill-in-the-blank bookmarks, or other handouts before, during, or after the presentation. Many of our presentations are only demonstrations, so we try to keep the students involved by asking lots of questions. If the presentation is in a lab, we do a brief demonstration before letting the students use the resource on their own. Before leaving, we quickly review the resource and remind them how they can return to it later on.

Insights & Improvements

Always have a "canned" presentation as backup. Sometimes your Internet connection won't work, but if you've saved some screen shots on a disk, at least you'll have something to show the audience. We sometimes put the screen shots into PowerPoint.

A lot of students think that "the Web has everything," and that they don't need to use books, magazines, or other resources anymore. When introducing a Web-based resource, it's a good idea to mention right at the beginning what it's good for (such as current events or recent research) and what it's not good for (lengthy information).

Use applicable examples. If students don't have a reason to use the resource, they often won't remember it when they *do* have a reason. If their next report or research project is looming, the information will seem much more interesting. Ask questions of the students and try to make your presentation as interactive as possible.

Kids might be technology savvy but not information savvy. A lot of adults talk about students' ability to learn technology quickly. Although *some* students catch on to the use of technology more quickly than adults, they still need help with information skills. A lot of our presentations focus on when to use certain kinds of resources as opposed to others and on how to find the *best* information within a particular resource.

Contact Person

Jackie Partch, School Corps Team Leader
Multnomah County Library
205 NE Russell
Portland, OR 97212
(503) 988-6004
jacquelp@nethost.multnomah.lib.or.us

WEB PAGE FOR WHAT WOULD YOU LIKE TO KNOW ABOUT INDIANA?

MONROE COUNTY PUBLIC LIBRARY, INDIANA

CHILDREN'S SERVICES, www.monroe.lib.in.us/childrens/childrens_dept.html

Overview

The Monroe County Community School Corporation is well connected. While students in some schools have greater access to computers than others, every school is connected to the Internet. Increasingly, students are expecting to find information on the Internet about their research topics.

The following report describes the Web page and program the children's librarians at the Monroe County Public Library developed to introduce Internet resources to students studying the state of Indiana.

Program Title

What Would You Like to Know About Indiana?
www.monroe.lib.in.us/childrens/tourin.html

Target Audience

Fourth grade students in the Monroe County Community School Corporation.
(*Reported by Lisa Champelli, children's librarian, Monroe County Public Library*)

Required Equipment

A computer with Internet access, a Web browser, and a projector are needed. Because we conduct this program for classes that average 20 to 25 students, we reserve the library's LitePro projector for use in the children's department program room. (The projector is connected to a computer that can access the Internet when plugged in

---

Figure 2-9: The Web-based research guide Monroe County Public Library developed encourages students to begin their research with a question.

Children's Services - *Monroe County Public Library, Indiana - (812) 349-3100*
Booklists   Search Tools   Web Sites   Program Schedule

What Would You Like to Know about Indiana?

Go to the next page to take Indiana Tour ... - Go to List of Websites about Indiana...

Return to Children's Services

---

to the library's network. The computer and projector are housed on a cart with wheels so that they can easily be moved to various rooms throughout the library.) We set up chairs in the room, facing the wall where the computer screen will be displayed. The librarian stands at the computer in the back of the room to demonstrate the Web page and navigate through some of the links.

Program Description

As part of their fourth grade curriculum, students in the Monroe County Community School Corporation research their great state of Indiana. Some teachers ask students to select a topic to examine in detail, and some teachers request that the MCPL children's librarians conduct a "research tour" for their class.

When a fourth grade class visits the library for the Indiana research tour, a children's librarian introduces students to the collection of books and reference materials available in the children's department to help them learn about the state of Indiana. (We also introduce them to the Indiana Room, a separate collection in the Monroe County Public Library, supervised by librarians with special knowledge of resources that provide information about local and state history.)

We take time to demonstrate how to use the library's online catalog to search for materials in the library, and how to use other electronic resources in our collection to find magazine articles, encyclopedia articles, pictures, and other information that might add to the students' knowledge of the topic they are researching.

Our goal is to familiarize students with the different methods they have for finding information in various formats that can help them learn about their topic. Because many students expect to find information on the Internet about their topic, we started suggesting Internet resources they might find useful as well.

We generally allow at least two hours for a research tour so that we can have about 45 minutes for instruction, 15 minutes to tour the children's department and visit the Indiana Room, and 60 minutes for the students to spend finding materials and taking notes.

We have a lot to explain in 45 minutes, and we need to concentrate on teaching students how to find materials in the library because that is the main objective of their class time with us. Yet we also wanted to provide some direction for finding information on the Internet that might help them when they were continuing their research at school or home.

Developing the "What Would You Like to Know about Indiana?" Web page enabled us to start our instructional presentation in a visually engaging manner that concludes with the reminder that the local library may be the best source of information.

In preparation for the class visits for the Indiana research tour, individual librarians had been writing down URLs of Web sites to share with students. Although we emphasize that the library's collection of print materials might have the best information on their research topic, we were finding that some students were choosing topics that our print collection did not address very well. For example, many students wanted to get current information about sports teams or individual college athletes. Often the team's Web site provided just the kind of statistical information the student wanted, or biographical information on team players.

One librarian had been bookmarking sites she wanted to remember to share with students, but the bookmarked list was saved to the computer at our reference desk and not accessible from the computer we used for class presentations. We had also been preparing handouts of recommended Web sites for students to take with them.

In 1999, I created a Web page listing useful Web sites to share with students looking for information about Indiana. I started with the bookmarked list of sites and others that librarians had been recommending, and added sites that served as indexes for Indiana topics.

Because we knew we would be referring to this page in the instruction about how to find information on Indiana topics, we de-

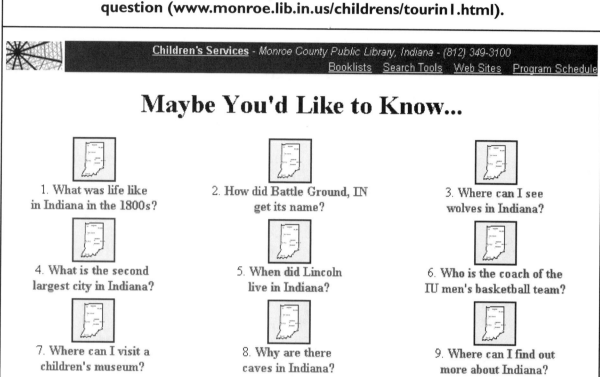

Figure 2-10: The links above each question lead to a Web site that answers the question (www.monroe.lib.in.us/childrens/tourin1.html).

cided to create other Web pages that we could use as a sort of slide show for our presentation.

The opening Web page, "What Would You Like to Know about Indiana?" (www.monroe.lib.in.us/childrens/tourin.html), helps to focus students' attention on the topic at hand. The next page, "Maybe You'd Like to Know . . .," serves to introduce some of the individual Web sites they might find that can add to their knowledge of a topic. Each link leads to a Web site that can help answer a question a student might have about Indiana. This presentation helps illustrate that our study of a topic usually begins with a question.

The bottom half of this page includes source information, which provides brief annotations of the featured Web sites and the answer to the question listed under each link. On occasion, an additional URL is included to indicate what page on the site actually provides the answer to the question. This helps us remind students that sometimes you have to read through different sections of a Web site to find the answer you are looking for. Even though the information doesn't appear on the opening page, that doesn't mean it's not there. Some annotations also refer to books that a student might consult for a direct answer to the question.

The last question on this page leads to the bibliography of sites about Indiana and a reminder that the library is a good place for students to start their research. This offers a nice transition for our instruction on how to use the library's online catalog.

Insights & Improvements

We're always working to find the best way to present research strategies to students so they leave the library feeling confident about their abilities to find the information they need.

Part of our job is to anticipate questions from students and identify in advance materials that will contain the answers to their questions. But we also want students to learn how to find materials on their own. This program tries to achieve both those goals. We wanted this Web presentation to be something that would be helpful to use with students year after year. For this reason, the bibliography of sites about Indiana emphasizes general Web sites that serve as indexes to finding information about more specific topics, or that can lead to specific information to answer questions about Indiana.

Of course, even metasites disappear. We regularly have to check the Web sites we link to, to make sure that the URL hasn't changed or that the annotated content is the same. But this is something we would have to do even if we just handed students a printed Webliography. The Web administrator for the library runs link-checking software on the site as a whole on a regular basis, prints a list of URLs that received error messages, and distributes to me the list of URLs I am responsible for checking. It helps to have a prepared list of URLs that need correction, but I still need to check each individual site and update the address, if indeed it was in error.

Sometimes Web sites are dismaying to students who expect to have the answer they're looking for pop up immediately. We make sure to explain how to navigate a site and emphasize that just as with print materials, obtaining information from an Internet source is going to require *reading* and *thinking*.

Contact

Lisa Champelli, Children's Librarian
Monroe County Public Library
303 East Kirkwood
Bloomington, IN 47408
(812) 349-3100
lchampel@monroe.lib.in.us

Chapter 3

Summer Reading Programs

According to the American Library Association, 95 percent of public libraries in the United States offer a summer reading program to school-age children. ALA states that these programs have proven to be "the most important factor in avoiding the decline in reading skills educators refer to as 'summer learning loss'" (1998).

Traditionally, summer reading programs offer some sort of incentive to encourage children to read. Some libraries encourage kids to read a certain number of books; others choose to reward kids for the length of time they spend reading. With the increasing availability of the Internet, more and more libraries are adding Web-based components to their summer reading programs as an additional means to engage young people in reading and literacy-related activities and to encourage use of the library and its resources.

The Web also provides a means to publicize the program, and enables kids to register for and participate in the program even if they are not able to come into the library.

As Walter Minkel, technology editor for *School Library Journal*, noted in a *NetConnect* supplement, "Summer (and year-round) reading programs in libraries . . . loom as an area ripe for technological innovation. A library tracking hundreds—and in big systems, many thousands—of young readers needs to lose the big boxes of paper game boards and provide a quick solution for the child who comes up to the desk saying, 'I've lost (or forgotten) my game board. Can I still get my prize?'" (2000: 43).

Minkel, who worked as a School Corps technology trainer for Multnomah County Public Library in Oregon until April 1999, certainly knows it can be done. Librarians at Multnomah County started providing online registration for their summer reading program in 1998.

Although it is a large library system with perhaps more staff resources than many libraries have, Multnomah County's methods are replicable by smaller libraries. If you're not yet ready to move your registration online but you would like ideas for how to integrate use of the Web in your summer reading program, you'll find examples of how to do just that from the following libraries featured in this section:

- Monroe County Public Library, Indiana
- Multnomah County Public Library, Oregon
- Daughin County Library System, Pennsylvania
- Carmel Clay Public Library, Indiana
- Timberland Regional Public Library, Washington

WHERE IN THE WORLD IS INDIANA JOAN AND COMPUTER COMET QUIZ WEB-BASED GAMES

MONROE COUNTY PUBLIC LIBRARY, INDIANA

CHILDREN'S DEPARTMENT, www.monroe.lib.in.us/childrens/childrens_dept.html

Overview

Since Monroe County Public Library's children's department began providing public Internet access in 1998, it has featured Web sites of the month on its Web page (www.monroe.lib.in.us/childrens/childrens_webmonth.html).

The Web sites are chosen by one of the children's librarians to help promote sites of special interest to kids (and/or their parents and teachers) and those that might relate to current events or seasonal topics. We incorporated this method for directing kids to appealing, age-appropriate Web sites into the site we develop to help promote our summer reading program. Of course, our other motive is to provide kids with another opportunity for reading! The following report describes the first Web-based activity we designed for our 1998 summer reading program, images created for the 2000 summer reading

---

Figure 3-1: The homepage for the summer reading program refers children to both recommended books and Web sites.

MCPL Children's Services
1998 Summer Reading Program

A World of Adventures!

Program Schedule

Websites: *Where in the World is Indiana Joan?*

Booklists for all ages

Click on the picture to find out where Joan has landed!

Return to Children's Services

---

program Web site, and how we made our Web-based activity a more integral part of our program in 2001.

Program Title

A World of Adventures—1998 Summer Reading Program
Note: The 1998 site is no longer available to the public. The 2001 summer reading program is available at www.monroe.lib.in.us/childrens/2001trailblazer.html. The Web site affiliated with MCPL's most current summer reading program can be found at www.monroe.lib.in.us/childrens/childrens_progsched.html.

Target Audience

School-age children through grade six.
(*Reported by Lisa Champelli, MCPL children's librarian*)

Required Equipment

Users need access to the Internet and a Web browser.

Figure 3-2: Selected Web sites are related to weekly themes.

MCPL Children's Services

Where in the World Is Indiana Joan?

Indiana Joan seeks adventures around the world! Find out where in the world she has landed this week, by clicking on the right answer to the question about the place she is visiting! Where did she go during...

1: Kick-off Week!

3: Worldwide Wildlife Week

5: Global Games Week

7: Extraterrestrial Week

2: International Intrigue Week

4: Passport to the Past Week

6: Continental Capers Week

8: Wrap-up Week

Return to A World of Adventures!

Program Description

As part of its summer reading program, MCPL encourages children to visit the library on a weekly basis over the summer and earn a prize for completing a literacy activity. (Children who have completed kindergarten and first grade must answer a question about a rebus story. Children who have completed second through sixth grade must decipher a secret message using a predetermined code the librarians have explained to them.) In 1998, the children's librarians decided to extend their weekly invitations to visit the library, encouraging kids to explore the library's Web site too.

The opening page for the summer reading program included links to the program schedule, which provides dates and times for special events and activities happening in the library over the summer, a bibliography highlighting books related to our weekly themes, and a list of Web sites also related to the weekly themes. The Web site listings were part of a Web-based game we created, "Where in the World Is Indiana Joan?" (Yes, we borrow shamelessly from games, television programs, movies, and other popular culture that we believe will resonate with or engage the kids we serve.)

Kids discovered the Web sites for the week when they clicked on the right answer to the clues that suggested where Indiana Joan was visiting that week. For example, during Worldwide Wildlife Week, the clue stated: "This is a land of contrasts, with both tropical rainforests and dry deserts. You'll find the world's largest desert here, as well as the world's longest river. You'll also find valuable minerals, such as diamonds and gold—and beautiful animals, too. Elephants,

---

Figure 3-3: After reading the clue, children click on the link to find out if they chose the right answer.

MCPL Children's Services

(3) Worldwide Wildlife Week:

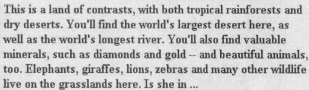

Where in the World Is Indiana Joan?
This is a land of contrasts, with both tropical rainforests and dry deserts. You'll find the world's largest desert here, as well as the world's longest river. You'll also find valuable minerals, such as diamonds and gold -- and beautiful animals, too. Elephants, giraffes, lions, zebras and many other wildlife live on the grasslands here. Is she in ...

Arkansas OR Africa

Return to A World of Adventures!

---

giraffes, lions, zebras and many other wildlife live on the grasslands here." There were two possible answers that kids could choose: Arkansas or Africa.

When they clicked on the word Arkansas, the corresponding Web page read:

> "Sorry—Try Again!
> "Arkansas is a beautiful land of thick forests and fertile plains—and you can even find valuable diamonds in this state. But it's known for its large, rejuvenating hot springs, not for having the world's largest desert. You can read more about Arkansas in *World Book Encyclopedia* or in books about Arkansas. Look for books on the blue shelves in the Children's Department with the call number 917.67. (Did you know our President, Bill Clinton, is from Arkansas?) You can also find Web sites about Arkansas. See: Stately Knowledge—Arkansas or Welcome to Arkansas."

This page also encouraged kids to go back and try again, with a hypertext link back to the clue page for that week, giving them another chance to choose the right answer.

Kids who clicked on "Africa" were rewarded with the greeting on the corresponding page that stated: "Good Job—That's the Right Answer!"

Figure 3-4: Children can return to the previous page to choose the correct answer.

MCPL Children's Services

Where in the World Is Indiana Joan?

Sorry - Try Again!

Arkansas is a beautiful land of thick forests and fertile plains - and you can even find valuable diamonds in this state. But it's known for its large, rejuvenating hot springs, not for having the world's largest desert. You can read more about Arkansas in *World Book Encyclopedia* or in books about Arkansas. Look for books on the blue shelves in the Children's Department with the call number 917.67. (Did you know our President, Bill Clinton, is from Arkansas?) You can also find web sites about Arkansas. See:

Stately Knowledge - Arkansas or

Welcome to Arkansas

Go Back and Try Again

Here they also found a little more information about Africa, a link to a Web page that could tell them more about the continent, and links to Web sites we selected that provided information about wildlife, the theme for the week.

The development of the summer reading program's theme and materials is a collaborative process. We usually have our theme in place by late fall so that we have time to develop and coordinate our materials around it. When possible, we like to have the same images appear in our print materials, in the promotional video, and on the Web.

We strive for simple, clean Web pages that will not frustrate users who have slow Internet connections or older browsers. While I hope to incorporate more animated and interactive elements to our Web pages for kids, the "keep it simple" approach has worked well for the time being, especially since I fit the creation of Web pages for MCPL's children's services in with my reference, selection, programming, and other responsibilities as a children's librarian. Plus, my Web design skills are pretty basic. Although I'm familiar with various HTML editors, I manually code my Web pages using the Unix system pico editor to ensure that the HTML code will meet the standards for the MCPL Web site as a whole, established by MCPL's Web Committee.

Figure 3-5: Selected Web sites lead children to more information about Indiana Joan's location or the weekly theme.

MCPL Children's Services

Where in the World Is Indiana Joan?

Good Job – That's the Right Answer!

The second largest continent, Africa, is home to the Sahara, the world's largest desert, and the Nile, the world's longest river. You can read more about Africa in *World Book Encyclopedia*, in books (look for the call number 916) and on the World Wide Web! See:

Africa Online - Kids Only!

Then - try out these wildlife sites:

Wild Egypt: On-line Safari

Kratts' Creatures

The Raptor Center

National Wildlife Foundation

Return to Where in the World is Indiana Joan

Fortunately, I have some very talented coworkers to call on for assistance. The drawings of Indiana Joan were created by Joshua Johnson, who was MCPL's graphic artist at the time. He was able to save his work as .gif files so that we could use his illustrations on the Web. Occasionally, I seek assistance from our Web administrator, Paula Gray-Overtoom, to resize graphic images so they will not take too long to download when they appear on a Web page. I do use images from free clip art sites to illustrate our Web pages, but I much prefer to use original artwork created for MCPL when possible, as this gives our pages a unique identity.

For example, in 2000, our graphic artist Ellen Sieber scanned photographs of the children's librarians and then incorporated a face with a cartoonlike body she found in an old 1950s advertisement. She combined the elements using Adobe Photoshop image editing software to manipulate the image sections in separate layers. This feature in Photoshop (one of its most useful ones, Ellen says) enables her to adjust how an image appears by flipping it from side to side, altering its position, and so on. She then filled in the lines and modified the drawings as necessary using Photoshop's paintbrush tool. Finally, she compressed the layers of the image and saved the composite pictures as .jpg images for use on the Web.

Figure 3-6: Graphics for MCPL's Summer Reading 2000 Web pages combined clip art with photographs of the children's librarians' faces for a fun effect (www.monroe.lib.in.us/childrens/knowit2000.html).

Children's Services - *Monroe County Public Library, Indiana - (812) 349-3100*
          Booklists   Search Tools   Web Sites   Program Schedule

Welcome to MCPL Children's Services'
Summer Reading 2000:
Your Year 2 Know!

What would you like to know today?

- **What is the Summer Reading Program?**
  (http://www.monroe.lib.in.us/childrens/srp2000.html)
- **What programs are happening each week?**
  Nature Investigators! Try the **Weed Identification** site!
  Two results from the **Create a Web Page** program!
- **What is the Weekly Challenge Code?**
  (http://www.monroe.lib.in.us/childrens/code.html)
- **How do I solve the code?**
  (http://www.monroe.lib.in.us/childrens/codehow.html)
- **What are the categories for the**
  Read a Million Books game?
- **What are the Weekly Web Sites?**

Return to **Children's Services**

We were thrilled to have the smiling face of the children's department manager on the opening page for the summer reading program site to help associate our Web site with the work of the children's department!

Insights & Improvements

I find it helpful to prepare the Web sites for our summer reading program as far in advance as possible. Once the program begins in June, it's hard to find time to do anything else except help register kids and prepare for that week's events.

Because the weekly themes for our 1998 *World of Adventure* were all determined months in advance, I had plenty of time to choose which Web sites we wanted to feature each week, research information for the clues, and write the text for each page. I was able to prepare the markup for each week's pages and have them all ready to go. I wouldn't activate the link to a week's pages until the start of that particular week.

The statistics from our Web server reports showed that we did have

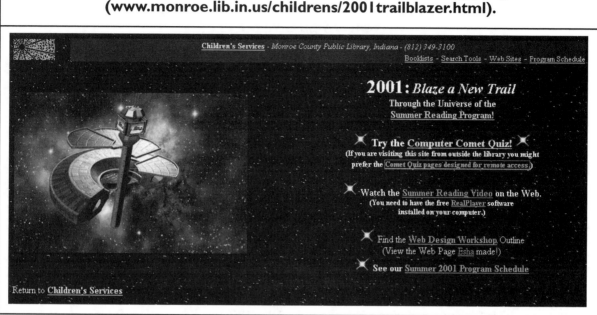

Figure 3-7: Homepage for MCPL's 2001 summer reading program (www.monroe.lib.in.us/childrens/2001trailblazer.html).

people visiting the summer reading program Web pages each year, but we were never sure if these were visits from kids who were participating in the program. While our Web site aims to help us connect with kids both inside and outside the library, whether or not they are participating in the summer reading program, we decided to promote the use of our Web site more in the 2001 program by making it one of the activities for which a child could receive credit.

As part of the 2001 *Blaze a New Trail* program, kids played a Web game similar to "Where in the World Is Indiana Joan?" But this year, they wrote down the correct answer to the Web-based Computer Comet Quiz (www.monroe.lib.in.us/childrens/2001trailblazer.html) in their summer reading "Star Charts" to record their use of our Web site as a completed activity that counted toward their overall participation in the program.

Children who came into the library to register for the summer reading program received a trifold brochure that contained a chart where they attached stickers to record activities they completed. In addition to finding and writing down the answer to the weekly Comet Quiz question, children could earn stickers, worth one point each, for reading a book, listening to an audiobook, playing a CD-ROM game or story, attending a library program, solving the weekly secret code, or answering the weekly rebus story question. Children earned prizes when they accumulated 5, 15, and 25 points.

We try to keep the Comet Quiz questions fairly short and targeted at a third grade reading level. (Beginning readers could ask a parent

Figure 3-8: The Web-based activity for MCPL's 2001 summer reading program featured short quiz questions (www.monroe.lib.in.us/childrens/ remcometquiz3.html).

Figure 3-9: The correct answer revealed recommended Web sites to explore, as well as the grinning alien mascot (designed by multimedia artist John Ward) for MCPL's 2001 summer reading program (www.monroe.lib.in.us/childrens/ remcometquiz3a.html).

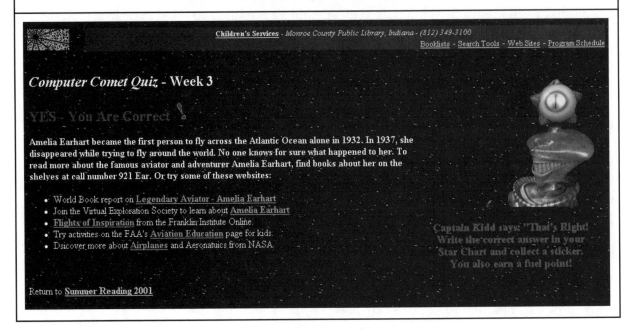

or other caregiver to read the question with them.) Kids can easily recognize whether they have selected the correct answer by the "YES!" or "Sorry!" that appears at the top of the next page. Our goal isn't to stump kids, but to help reinforce something they might already know, help them discover something new, or learn how to find out more about a topic that interests them. The explanations we provide to each possible answer are meant to help satisfy the truly curious. Often, the explanation includes the Dewey decimal number for locating books on the featured subject, and on occasion we noticed children (or a parent) who wrote down the Dewey number in the margin of their Star Charts so they could go to the library shelves and find some books to take home.

Besides encouraging use of our Web site, using the Star Chart to record visits to the Computer Comet Quiz pages enabled children's librarians to talk with kids about our Web site and learn more about how they like using it as part of our summer reading program. We found that some children did not use the Web site at all. But feedback we received during the summer and from surveys completed by parents whose children participated in the reading program indicated that many families felt the Comet Quiz Web activity was a valuable component of the summer reading program. Many appreciated that the quiz questions remained up all summer so that kids who were out of town for part of the summer could either access them remotely or access previous weeks' questions when they returned.

We plan to revise the structure of our reading program a little for 2002 (so that we aren't so overwhelmed with requests for stickers!), but we will keep the Comet Quiz or a similar Web-based activity as one of the literacy activities kids can choose to do at the library.

Contact Person

Lisa Champelli, Children's Librarian
Monroe County Public Library
303 East Kirkwood
Bloomington, IN 47408
(812) 349-3100
lchampel@monroe.lib.in.us

TICKET TO TOMORROW WEB PAGE AND ONLINE REGISTRATION

MULTNOMAH COUNTY PUBLIC LIBRARY, OREGON

YOUTH SERVICES KIDS PAGE, www.multcolib.org/kids/index.html

Overview

Multnomah County Public Library's Youth Services encourages kids to register online for the summer reading program. The following report describes their online registration and how they incorporated the use of the Web into other elements of their 2000 summer reading program.

Program Title

Summer Reading 2000: Ticket to Tomorrow
www.multnomah.lib.or.us/lib/summer

Target Audience

Multnomah County Library's *Ticket to Tomorrow* summer reading program targets youth from birth through age 18. The Web site targets school-age children, with sections directed toward grade school, middle school, and teens.
(*Reported by Youth Services Librarian Erica Moore in collaboration with Youth Services Coordinator Ellen Fader and Youth Services Librarians Kate Carter and Jennifer Fox*)

Required Equipment

Access to the Internet, a Web browser, and a printer to output the game board.

Figure 3-10: Homepage for Multnomah County's 2000 summer reading program (www.multnomah.lib.or.us/lib/summer/2000/menu.html).

Program Description

Rules for the Multnomah County's summer reading program appeared on the library's Web site, available at www.multnomah.lib.or.us/lib/summer/srrules.html.

You can play Ticket to Tomorrow in three ways: Read To Me, Read On My Own, and Young Adult (called Teen Game in 2001). Everyone receives the same game board, but the activities are a little different for each age group. For example, guidelines for the Read On My Own age group (readers up to grade six) state:

1. For every 30 minutes that you read, color in one of the rockets on your game board. (Readers may also count the times someone reads to them.)

2. Once you have colored in the tenth rocket on a level, you may bring your game board to the library and choose a prize.
3. For each prize level (at the Read on My Own level) you may substitute one of the following activities for one 30-minute period of reading:

*   Have a friend sign up for the summer reading game.
*   Attend a library program.
*   Explore one of the programs on the children's CD-ROM station.
*   Listen to a book on cassette or CD.
*   Locate the Multnomah County Library Web page for kids, KidsPage.
*   Watch a video based on a book.
*   Write a book review for the library's summer reading Web site. (You may also ask for a form at the library.)
*   Read aloud to someone else.
*   Participate in a Multnomah County Library summer reading Web page activity.
*   Check out a CD-ROM and use it at home.
*   Visit the David Wiesner exhibit at the Central Library.

Kids must visit the library in order to claim prizes, continue in the summer reading program, and advance to the next prize level. However, because the online registration page for the program and the start-up game board appear on the Web, kids are able to begin and participate in the program without having to visit the library.

Signing up online offers our customers options and expands our program. By using the Internet and allowing kids to begin the program online, we can meet the needs of a larger audience (people with disabilities, scheduling conflicts, transportation issues, and so on). Summer reading online registration and activities on the Web allow us to expand outside of the physical building and reach kids.

Summer reading begins while the kids are still in school. The summer reading game is promoted in schools to kids in May and early June. Youth services staff members explain the game and tell kids about the Web site. Kids can access the summer reading page inside the library from any Internet station or outside the library on the Web. Some schools sign kids up online.

Kids currently access Multnomah County Library resources from the schools via our Web pages for recreational or homework purposes. We work hard to have a strong partnership with our schools and have a history of going into the schools to present book talks and other programs. It seems a natural step to allow kids to sign up and begin the summer reading program at school via the Internet and the summer reading page.

It's important to reach kids on the Web and provide appropriate activities and information for them on the Internet. The summer reading Web page offers educational and recreational sites and activities. The page helps to promote what we already do inside the library building as well as online: provide educational and recreational materials and activities to our community. It also helps establish and maintain our presence on the Web with our community.

Several Web pages are featured components of Multnomah's summer reading program:

- The opening splash page with the program logo, www.multnomah.lib.or.us/lib/summer, links to the index page where program information and activities can be found.
- The online registration page, www.multnomah.lib.or.us/lib/summer/srreg.html, is a forms page that a volunteer created for the library. After August 31, 2000, the coding for the registration form was commented out of the HTML code so that no one could attempt to register after the program had concluded. But while active, it stated:

You can register for Ticket to Tomorrow, the library's summer reading game, on the computer.

1. Fill out this online registration form and submit it.
   Please check with a parent or other adult before sending your name or any other information about you to anyone on the Internet. The names of Multnomah County Library summer readers who register on the Internet are not released to the public; the information is used for statistical purposes only.
2. When the game board appears on your computer screen, print it.
   The game board should appear when you click on the "SIGN ME UP!" button. You must be able to print from your computer to start playing Ticket to Tomorrow.
3. Start reading. Use your game board to keep track of your reading.
4. Bring your game board to your neighborhood library for prizes!
   *You **must** bring your filled-out game board to any Multnomah County library to get credit for the books you have read.*

The online registration form itself was a series of boxes with various questions. Children were directed to use the tab key or the mouse to move between the questions, asking:

- Which Multnomah County library do you use most? (Registrants could select from a listing of Multnomah County libraries.)
- Your first and last name
- Your age
- Your grade in fall 2000
- Your school name next fall
- Is your school outside of Multnomah County?
- What kind of school is it? (Check one.)
  Preschool
  Elementary
  Middle
  High
- Which game will you play? (Check one.)
  Read to Me
  Read on My Own
  Young Adult
- Did you play the reading game last summer?
  Yes   No
- Where did you hear about Summer Reading? (Check one.)
  School
  Library
  Web
  Parent/Friend
  Ads/Billboard

Once the registrant completes the form by typing in the requested information or selecting the appropriate category, the registrant clicks on the "Sign Me Up!" button, and the information is e-mailed to a designated librarian. A follow-up page appears stating, "Thanks for registering for Summer Reading!" This page also reviews how to participate.

The rules state:

You may start playing now by following these steps.

1. Review the game rules.
   When you finish reading or printing* the rules, click on the BACK button on your browser to return to this page. (*HINT: When the rules appear on your computer screen, you can print them by clicking on your browser's PRINT button.)
2. Get your start-up game board.
   Click here to view a game board on your computer screen that you can print. When the game board appears on your computer screen, print it by clicking on your browser's PRINT button.

Figure 3-11: The page listing the rules for Multnomah's summer reading program lets participants know where they can find their first game board on the Web (www.multcolib.org/summer/srgame.html).

 Multnomah County Library *Summer Reading 2000*

Home

Sign Up

Books

Book Groups

Crafts & Games

Events

Jokes

Links

Teens

About

Prizes

Rules

Thanks for registering for Summer Reading!

You may start playing now by following these steps.

1. **Review the game rules.**
   When you finish reading or printing* the rules, click on the BACK button on your browser to return to this page.
   (*HINT: When the rules appear on your computer screen, you can print them by clicking on your browser's PRINT button.)

2. **Get your start-up gameboard.**
   Click here to view a gameboard on your computer screen that you can print. When the gameboard appears on your computer screen, print it by clicking on your browser's PRINT button.

3. Read books and mark off the spaces on your start-up gameboard.

4. Once you have marked off the 10th space, bring your start-up gameboard to the library, choose a prize and pick up your official gameboard so you can keep playing.

Ticket to Tomorrow Home | **Library Home**

3. Read books and mark off the spaces on your start-up game board.
4. Once you have marked off the 10th space, bring your start-up game board to the library, choose a prize, and pick up your official game board so you can keep playing

The actual game board for the 2000 summer reading program looked like the one in Figure 3-12.

In addition to the online registration pages and game board, the

Figure 3-12: Multnomah County children's librarians facilitate participation in their summer reading program by making the initial game board available on the Web.

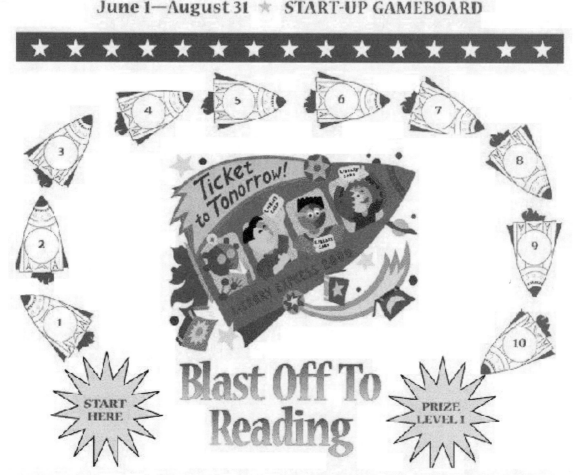

Ticket to Tomorrow pages included Web-based activities that counted toward a participant's cumulative reading goal.

We created a Web page for summer reading that incorporated Web activities into the summer reading program. Many of our youth access the computers in the library to find books, do homework, play games, or research hobbies. We have included normal library behavior and use into the summer reading program—i.e., using the Internet or CD-ROMs during a visit to the library, as well as checking out books.

The activities on the *Ticket to Tomorrow* pages are tied to the summer reading theme. There is a mix of educational and recreational sites for children to explore over the summer.

We have book suggestions, book reviews, games, crafts, and activities online. Kids are encouraged to participate in the online activities by receiving credit on their reading game board. But the summer reading game is self-directed, both the reading and the Web parts of the game. It is up to the child to choose to participate in a Web activity.

- At www.multnomah.lib.or.us/lib/summer/srreview.html#form, kids could submit online book reviews and read other reviews. Writing a review also counted as an activity on their game boards. I found that kids like the online book reviews. It is important not to "clean up" the review written by the child. Keeping the personalities and the styles of the children is more important than what they actually wrote. They feel important being on the Web. I only put up first names and ages. They know who they are.
- At www.multnomah.lib.or.us/lib/summer/srcrafts.html, summer readers could try out games and activities and receive credit on their game boards.

We choose sites based on age appropriateness, interest to children, and connection to the summer reading theme. Some activities on the page were created by staff, others are links to nonlibrary pages. In addition, children have the option of online activities on the Outernet, the Web page for eighth grade and up (www.multnomah.lib.or.us/lib/outer/index.html).

They could also visit the Multnomah County Library's KidsPage, www.multnomah.lib.or.us/lib/kids/index.html, geared to young children and school-age children through eighth grade, where they could engage in more online activities and credit their summer reading game boards.

DESIGNING THE *TICKET TO TOMORROW* WEB PAGES

The Oregon Library Association Summer Reading Committee develops a summer reading manual with activities, programs, and clip art, Moore reports. This manual is based on the statewide summer reading theme. Many ideas for activities on the Web page were taken from the manual. Often these ideas need to be translated into something that can become an activity on the Web.

The Multnomah County Summer Reading Committee then designs a game for the library. The game at Multnomah County is unique but based on the statewide theme.

The Oregon Library Association pays for summer reading graphics to be created for the state. The graphics for 2000 were purchased from the Wisconsin Library Association. Some graphics are also designed in-house for use on the pages. Some of the smaller graphics were actually cut out of the larger logo and used individually. (I used Fireworks, a type of Web page design and graphics production software, to do this).

Multnomah County designs its own summer reading Web page in-house. People who work on the pages at Multnomah County can all hand code HTML and use HTML editors. People use a variety of Web design software at the library, such as Arachnophilia, Dreamweaver, and Macromedia Fireworks.

Software is often the personal choice of the page designer. We don't use cascading style sheets or higher-end code. We do not want to exclude people who use older browsers. No extra plug-ins are used in the construction of the pages. Graphics are kept as small as possible to keep downloading time to a minimum. It is important to make the site accessible to a wide audience. We keep the Americans with Disabilities Act guidelines in mind when designing our sites.

Insights & Improvements

I've learned it is better to have a few really good sites or activities in a cleanly designed page than a lot of sites. More is not better. Kids (and adults) will find your page more useful and rate it better if you have fewer high-quality sites and activities. Having too many sites seems like information overload. People want to be provided with the best sites.

The summer reading page is always previewed to youth services and Multnomah County Library's Summer Reading Committee. Library staff members provide input and feedback regarding library pages. There is a lot of collaboration on Web pages and other projects at the library. I think this helps make a successful program.

Contact Person

Ellen Fader, Youth Services Coordinator
Multnomah County Library
205 NE Russell
Portland, OR 97212-3796
(503) 988-5408
ellenf@multcolib.org

DCLS KIDS' CORNER SUMMER READING GAMES

DAUGHIN COUNTY LIBRARY SYSTEM, PENNSYLVANIA

KIDS CORNER, www.dcls.org/w/c/

Overview

Daughin County Library System has provided an online component to its summer reading program since 1997. "We have a wonderful Webmaster who develops an Internet adventure [almost] each year," praises Linda Moffet, assistant youth services coordinator for DCLS. David Goudsward, former Web administrator for DCLS, produces the artwork for the different games he's helped create in collaboration with Moffet and other youth services librarians.

Program Title

DCLS Kids' Corner Summer Reading Games
www.dcls.org/w/c/games.html

Target Audience

School-age children
(Reported by David Goudsward, former DCLS Web administrator)

Required Equipment

Access to the Internet, a Web browser, and a printer to output the worksheet associated with the program are needed. We also offset print a supply of the worksheets for in-branch use to save wear and tear on the printers. The 2000 program relied on JavaScripts and animated graphics; previous programs did not.

Program Description

All three online programs are geared to coincide thematically with the statewide summer reading program. The theme of each year's

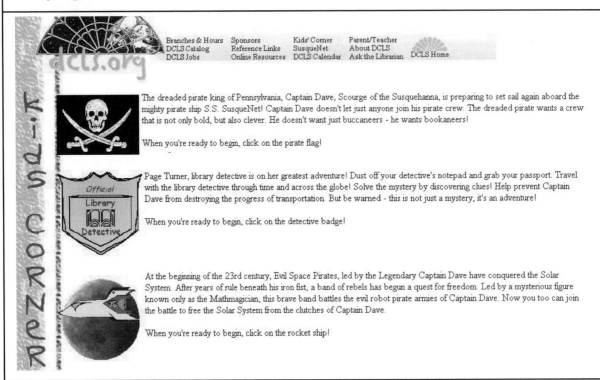

Figure 3-13: The Web-based games created for Daughin County's summer reading program are all available from the kids' section of the library's Web site.

summer reading program is developed cooperatively by librarians in a specific region of the state, under the auspices of the State Library.

The theme in 1997 was "Be a Bookaneer" and thus, the legend of Captain Dave was born. In 1999, "Route for Reading" brought Page Turner, Library Detective, to battle Captain Dave's attempt at destroying the history of transportation, and 2000's "Masters of the Millennium" sent Captain Dave into the future on a math adventure.

As kids navigate through the site, they answer questions on an answer sheet, then unscramble designated letters to answer a riddle. Local kids are directed to come to the library for a prize. Kids outside the local area have their names added to a participant list.

We tend to see more at-home completions of the online programs, but there is Internet access available at all eight of our branches. The online programs are available to anyone who wants to use them, but local participants (those who have registered for the summer reading programs at our branches) also have the option of turning in their worksheets to their local library for an additional prize. This year's prize, for example, was a geometric puzzle keychain.

The programs have three underlying goals:

Figure 3-14: Captain Dave's Treasure Hunt, part of the perpetually popular Pirate pages (http://dcls.org/pirate/pirate2.html)

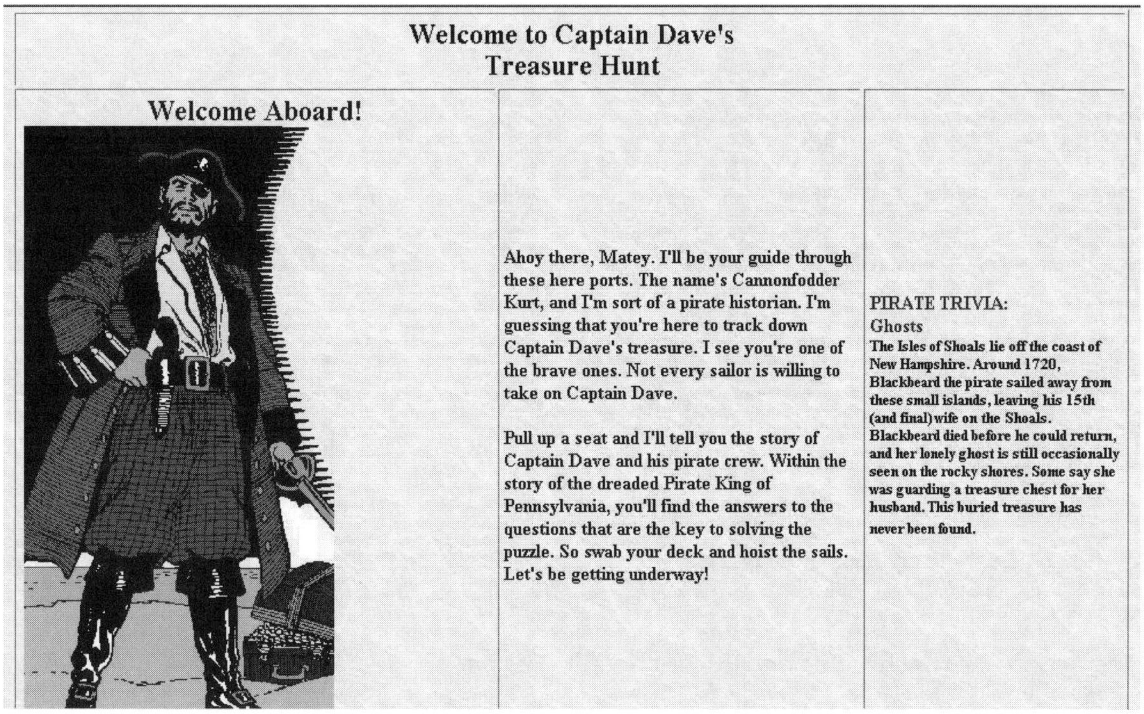

Welcome to Captain Dave's Treasure Hunt

Welcome Aboard!

Ahoy there, Matey. I'll be your guide through these here ports. The name's Cannonfodder Kurt, and I'm sort of a pirate historian. I'm guessing that you're here to track down Captain Dave's treasure. I see you're one of the brave ones. Not every sailor is willing to take on Captain Dave.

Pull up a seat and I'll tell you the story of Captain Dave and his pirate crew. Within the story of the dreaded Pirate King of Pennsylvania, you'll find the answers to the questions that are the key to solving the puzzle. So swab your deck and hoist the sails. Let's be getting underway!

PIRATE TRIVIA:
Ghosts
The Isles of Shoals lie off the coast of New Hampshire. Around 1720, Blackbeard the pirate sailed away from these small islands, leaving his 15th (and final) wife on the Shoals. Blackbeard died before he could return, and her lonely ghost is still occasionally seen on the rocky shores. Some say she was guarding a treasure chest for her husband. This buried treasure has never been found.

1. To create an environment where children (and adults) unfamiliar with basic Internet navigation skills can develop them.
2. To demonstrate that the Internet can be used as a research tool as well as an entertainment medium.
3. To provide links to materials that not only tie in with the adventure, but encourage additional exploration of a topic; that is, to encourage reading and learning for the sheer pleasure of doing so.

Once I know the theme for the year, I just start playing with it until something resonates. When I have that seed of an idea, I keep developing it, reassessing, and revising until I come up with something I think can be built on. The youth services staff (Linda Moffet in particular) usually bears the brunt of my thinking-out-loud process, which allows me to work things out and to bounce ideas off them. It is an ongoing process and I don't always end up where I expected. In fact, I don't usually have a clear idea what the ending will be until about halfway through the actual Web page construction process.

Figure 3-15: www.dcls.org/route/route14.html

Journal Entry #18
Limon Bay, Panama
August 15, 1914

As I expected, the ship Ancon was waiting at the lock, ready to become the first ship to officially use the <u>Panama Canal</u>. However, the massive gates of the Gatum Locks weren't opening. It looked like they were stuck. And I had a good idea who was behind it. I began looking for clues as to what Captain Dave had done to lock up the lock.

Whatever Captain Dave had done, it wasn't obvious. The motors looked good, there was plenty of power, the hinges were all fine, the controls were operational - the lock just wouldn't open. I looked down into the water - jackpot! There was something big and shiny up against the doors. I pulled my trusty Library Detective Underwater Investigation Kit out of the time machine and took a closer look...

Question Eight:
What was the original name of the Panama Canal's Gaillard Cut?

As I swam toward the lock, I suddenly realized the problem. Only Captain Dave would actually use a giant lock to lock a lock.

I didn't have a lockpick big enough to pick the lock of the lock locking the lock, and I was getting tired of saying the word "lock." It looked bad this time.

I decided to look at the problem logically. A giant lock needed a giant key. A giant key would be too big to carry, so Captain Dave had to have hidden it nearby.

I use HTMLEdit, which is basically Notepad with common HTML tags built on as function keys, to create the pages. The three Internet adventures actually have three very different approaches to graphics: "Pirates" used nautical clip art exclusively, "Route" featured digital photos of the administrative staff altered manually and dropped onto backgrounds, and "Masters" scanned in a young adult artist's inked images and then colored them. I rely heavily on the graphics design software Paint Shop Pro for creating .gifs (an image format) and for modifying and coloring graphics. I use Adobe PhotoDeluxe for resizing photographic quality .jpgs (another image format).

My favorite game, and the most successful, was the "Pirate" program, the continued popularity of which continues to amaze me.

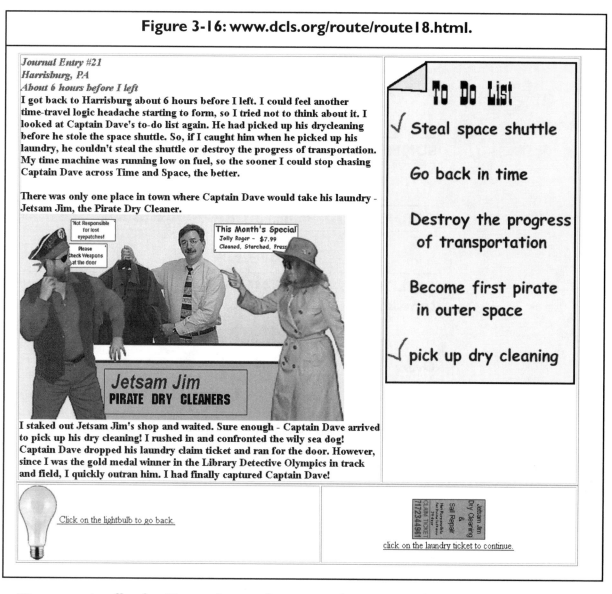

Figure 3-16: www.dcls.org/route/route18.html.

However, visually, the "Route for Reading" game has my two favorite images: the Panama Canal underwater shot and the climactic confrontation at the dry cleaner.

Insights & Improvements

Included on the companion Web site for the *Youth Cybrarian's Guide.*

Contact Persons

Dave Goudsward
webmaster@goudsward.com

Linda Moffet, Assistant Youth Services Coordinator
Dauphin County Library System
101 Walnut Street
Harrisburg, PA 17101
moffet@dcls.org

SUMMER STORY MYSTERY TALE ON THE WEB

CARMEL CLAY PUBLIC LIBRARY, INDIANA

CHILDREN'S DEPARTMENT, www.carmel.lib.in.us/child/chmain.htm

Overview

Daughin County Library System's Internet Adventures inspired Carmel Clay Children's Librarian Jennifer Andersen to develop a Web-based component to the library's summer reading program in 2000. Andersen explains why and how CCPL created the "Summer Story" Web site, how she and her colleagues revised the concept for the 2001 summer program, and their plans for improving the program in 2002.

Program Title

Summer Story
www.carmel.lib.in.us/child/story.htm (2000)
www.carmel.lib.in.us/child/story/chapter1.htm (2001)

Target Audience

School-age children
(Reported by Jennifer Andersen, children's librarian)

Required Equipment

Access to the Internet, a Web browser, and a printer to output the answer sheet

---

Figure 3-17: The *Summer Story* Carmel Clay children's librarians created as the Web-based activity for the 2000 summer reading program featured trickster characters from folklore.

 Carmel Clay Public Library Children's

Home | Audiovisual | Calendar | Catalog | Children's | Friends | Information | Reference | Young Adult

Summer Story

 It was a hot Spring day in Carmel, Indiana. Two tricksters, Coyote and Anansi the Spider (who was visiting from Africa) were basking in the sun telling each other about their various adventures. They were trying to decide which of them was the better trickster. "My last exploit was the best! I'm the one that brought fire to the People. Before the People had fire they were cold and unhappy. It definitely proves I'm a much better trickster than you!" said Coyote.

"Ah Coyote, that is a good tale, but I bought for the People all of Sky God's stories," said Anansi.

 "While you might own those stories, Anansi, I saved the Pomo People from a serious drought! I had to eat hundreds and hundreds of grasshoppers!" replied Coyote.

"We will never be able to decide which one of us is the better trickster until we put it to the test. I have an idea. Let's have a contest. Whoever wins will be declared the better trickster," said Anansi.

"Sounds good to me!" said Coyote. "What will we do?" Anansi whispered his idea to Coyote and Coyote broke out into gales of laughter. "You definitely have a crafty mind, Anansi. I like your idea. Let's begin now and see if these silly humans notice anything."

Program Description

Children read the *Summer Story* on the Web. The story explains the librarians' suspicions that the trickster characters Coyote and Anansi the Spider have stolen various children's literature characters from their favorite books and have sent them back in time. In order to rescue the missing characters, children must find the answers to the clues Coyote and Anansi left behind. The clues are linked to Web sites that children visit to find the answer to the clue question. They write the one-word answer in the blank spaces on the answer sheet. Each answer contains a circled letter. When children have obtained all the circled letters they can use them to determine the answer to a riddle. Once the riddle is solved, the characters are saved!

The Carmel Clay children's department was motivated to develop this Web-based activity by the "complaints" the department was getting each year from parents who felt that the summer reading program (SRP) was too short (the kids are required to read 16 hours in 8 weeks). Many of these parents want us to extend the program another two weeks until school starts. We are unable to do so because we need the time to prepare for our fall programs, and because our summer help returns to college.

In surfing the Web for pirate-related sites, I came across the DCLS (Dauphin County Library System) Web scavenger hunt "The Leg-

---

Figure 3-18: At the end of the *Summer Story*, children found the Web sites they would use to answer the questions and solve the mystery (www.carmel.lib.in.us/child/story.htm).

The next afternoon...

Professor Gladstone, scientist extraordinaire, was visiting the Carmel Library, putting the final touches on his Time Machine. He was donating it to the Children's Department for the summer as a special favor. It was going to be the centerpiece of their summer reading program, "Books: The Ultimate Time Machine." Suddenly Jennifer, one of the librarians, burst into the room.

"Professor Gladstone, you've got to help us! Someone has stolen Peter Rabbit right out of his books!" Jennifer yelled.

"What do you mean? Slow down! Start at the beginning," replied a shocked Professor Gladstone.

"I was showing a patron where the Peter Rabbit books are. I opened up one of the stories to show her some of the pictures, but Peter Rabbit disappeared right before our very eyes! All that was left behind was a paw print!" exclaimed Jennifer.

"A paw print? From what kind of animal?" asked Professor Gladstone.

"Here's the book. What do you think?" asked Jennifer.

"It looks like it's from a coyote. Was there anything else with the paw print?" asked Professor Gladstone.

"Yes, there was a dinosaur tattoo and a sheet of questions with weird circles around some of the blank spaces. At the bottom of the page is a riddle," replied Jennifer.

---

end of Captain Dave's Lost Treasure." I loved what they had done. It seemed to be a perfect way to extend our SRP for those dissatisfied parents and a great way to increase the use of and promote our Web site.

Once I presented the DCLS Web scavenger hunt to the children's department and explained my thoughts about doing something similar as a way to extend our SRP, we started discussing logistics. We wanted the page to be literature based, and we discussed several possible story lines. Gradually, the idea of incorporating traditional literature into the Web Scavenger Hunt, in the form of the tricksters Coyote and Anansi, was born. Their characteristic competitiveness lent itself to a contest structure, whereby they would argue over who was trickier. As folktale characters, they could and do "travel" through time, which fit with our time-travel theme.

Carmel Clay Public Library Computer Technology Coordinator Peter Konshak is responsible for the actual design of the library Web site. I am responsible for coordinating the children's department staff contributions to the site. Children's staff members proposing Web site content sit down with me to discuss their ideas for our Web page and I present these ideas to Peter. In this case, I presented examples from the DCLS Web site and explained to him our vision for the summer reading program page: what it should look like and how it should work.

Once Peter has an idea of what we want and determines if it is possible, I e-mail him a Microsoft Word document containing the text. I do very little editing (bold, italics, underlining) within this document. I also provide an edited hard copy to use as a template. I will also write in types of possible images and placement of those images. Once he has put together a mock-up, I go through the page and e-mail him any requested changes. We continue this dialogue until we are both happy with the results.

Insights & Improvements

One important element we did not take into consideration was breadth. Time travel was too broad a theme to fit the format we originally envisioned. We wanted the story to flow throughout the whole scavenger hunt, and we wanted the kids to have a chance to really learn about the different time periods. The number of time periods covered (eight) and the depth we wanted did not work with the amount of time available. Key points learned: Start early and start small! Focusing on just one time period would have been easier and allowed us to go into more depth.

Another big factor was publicity. Because the page took more time to create than expected, we launched it three weeks into our SRP, missing many opportunities to publicize this new aspect of the library's Web site through our SRP skit, brochures, room decorations, and so on. We didn't want to promote the Web page until it was up and running in case we ran into any glitches. Consequently, we did not have any kids participate. We think the largest contributing factor was this lack of publicity. For future programs, the Web scavenger hunt will be completely put together by May, and will be publicized in our SRP brochures, reading records, skit, summer reading room, and local newspapers. Motivation was another concern. The kids in our service respond well to external motivation. In putting the page together, we knew we needed to give them a reason (and reward) for completing the scavenger hunt. Originally, we thought adding their names to our Web site would be reward enough. We discussed moving to a token system, where participants receive one token for every hour they read. They will then be able to "spend"

their tokens in our Summer Reading Store. Our school-age participants will be able to earn an extra token if they complete the Web
scavenger hunt.

We definitely had much more success with *Summer Story 2*, "Case
of the Missing Books," than we did with our original *Summer Story*.
Most of this was due to the publicity and the incentive of earning an
extra token. Although we had more success, our numbers were still
relatively low. We only had 49 out of about 3,001 school-age kids finish the puzzles. They were much too hard and there were too many
of them. Several kids did the first few puzzles, but not many did the
last few. I think they got bored or felt all the work was not worth
one token. We do plan to continue this for 2002, but we will make it
a lot easier, as the majority of the kids participating are in the lower
elementary grades.

Contact Person

Jennifer Andersen, Children's Librarian
55 Fourth Avenue SE
Carmel, IN 46074
(317) 844-3363
jandersen@carmel.lib.in.us

JAMBOREAD AND TEENS REQUEST LIVE WEB-BASED REVIEW AND REQUEST FORMS

TIMBERLAND REGIONAL PUBLIC LIBRARY, WASHINGTON

TIMBERKIDS, www.timberland.lib.wa.us/kids.htm
TEEN ZONE, www.timberland.lib.wa.us/teens.htm

Overview

Timberland librarians chose to use forms on their summer reading
program Web pages as a way to communicate with children and
young adults about what they are reading and what kinds of materials they would like the library to purchase. In 2001, they added online
registration to their summer reading Web pages. (Check the Web

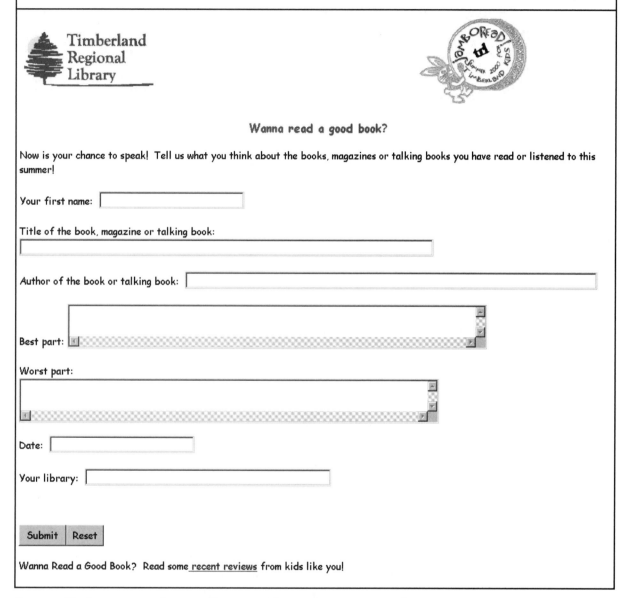

Figure 3-19: Timberland Regional Library included an online book review form as part of its summer reading program to encourage kids to describe books they had been reading. (www.timberland.lib.wa.us/srp00-good-book-form.htm).

Design Tools resource list in Chapter 5 for suggestions on where to learn more about creating forms for use on the Web.)

Program Title

JamboREAD
www.timberland.lib.wa.us/srp00-jamboread.htm
Teens Request Live
www.timberland.lib.wa.us/srp00-teens-request.htm

Figure 3-20: Timberland Regional Library invited teens to communicate with librarians via Web-based forms (www.timberland.lib.wa.us/srp00-teens-let-us-know-form.htm).

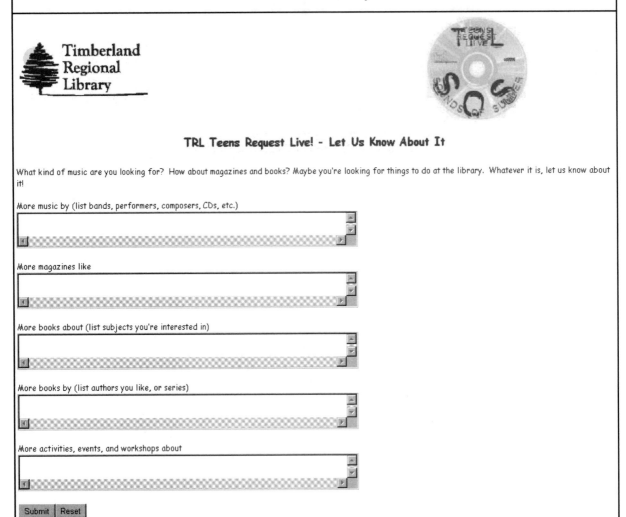

Target Audience

JamboREAD: Birth through those entering sixth grade
Teens Request Live: Entering 7th grade and up
(*Reported by Tiffany Tuttle, youth services librarian*)

Required Equipment

Access to the Internet and a Web browser

Program Description

The Timberland Regional Library posted information on its Summer Reading 2000 Web site (www.timberland.lib.wa.us/srp00-jamboread.htm) encouraging children to visit any Timberland Regional Library to pick up an entry brochure for *JamboREAD*, the summer reading program for children. Children use their entry brochures to record the titles of books, magazines, and books on tape or CD that they read or listen to, either independently or together with family or friends. Children then return their "JamboREAD" coupons to a Timberland library during specified dates of the summer reading program to claim their special one-time prize packet.

As a means for helping children find books to read, the Summer Reading Web site included a link to the "100 Favorite Children's Books" book list (www.timberland.lib.wa.us/srp00-100-good-books.htm) developed by the youth services staff of the Timberland Regional Library system.

Through the main page, youth service librarians also encourage kids to "Tell us about a great book to recommend to others!" and provide a link to the "Good Books Form" page (www.timberland.lib.wa.us/srp00-good-book-form.htm) where children can enter information about the books they've read. The page consists of blank boxes labeled with prompts suggesting the information to include in the review.

When a child clicked on the "Submit" button at the bottom of the page, the information they entered was sent as an e-mail message to a youth service librarian's e-mail account. The librarian then forwarded the e-mail message to the TRL Webmaster, who posted the submitted information on the library's "Wanna Read a Good Book?" response page (www.timberland.lib.wa.us/srp00-good-books.htm).

Timberland Library's main summer reading page features another online activity for kids, "Stump the Librarian." To play Stump the Librarian, children decide on a book, make up three clues about the book, and give the clues to a librarian. If the librarian cannot guess the name of the book, the child receives a sticker. Kids may receive one sticker each day they play.

Kids are encouraged to visit the library and challenge the librarian directly, but they can submit their "stumper" questions online via the "JamboREAD—Stump the Librarian" Web site (www.timberland.lib.wa.us/srp00-stump-form.htm).

Insights & Improvements

We feel these pages were successful, in that we received responses! This is a direction we want to continue working toward: offering kids and teens more ways to reach libraries and to contribute their ideas to our Web page, whether it be about a good book or a good Web site. Interactive pages were used again in 2001 (www.timberland. lib.wa.us/srp2001.htm) and will also join the regular Web pages permanently. In fact, in 2001 Timberland enabled kids to register online for the summer reading program via its Web page. The "Feed Your Brain: Sign Up Here for Summer Reading 2001" Web page is available at www.timberland.lib.wa.us/srp-2001-signup.htm.

My plans for improving the library's efforts to engage young people in library activities and services through the Web will focus on increasing publicity for the site. Next summer, we hope to print the summer reading Web page address on every piece of information we distribute in the hopes of reaching more people.

We want to make use of the medium and exploit all it has to offer. The immediacy of the Web makes updating information easy (such as info on local events). It's a natural community bulletin board. It is imperative to solicit teen and kid input often, determining what they want there and actually following through on it. Additionally, because all teens and kids are different, it is important to link to a wide variety of items. I also think that highlighting local content is important; many people can easily find large corporate pages themselves.

Timberland youth service librarians recommend useful Web sites and communicate with children and teens about ongoing library services and activities through the TimberKids page (www.timberland. lib.wa.us/kids.htm) and the Timberland TeenZone Page (www.timberland.lib.wa.us/teens.htm).

Contact Persons

Ellen Duffy, Youth Services Coordinator
Timberland Regional Library
eduffy@timberland.lib.wa.us.

Tiffany Tuttle, Youth Services Librarian
Lacey Timberland Library
ttuttle@timberland.lib.wa.us

Chapter 4

Recreational Programs

The recreational programming that public librarians provide for young people takes on many forms, extending opportunities for children and young adults to create, perform, discover, and learn. When the program includes the opportunity for the child to create something, the discovery becomes tangible. Whether the invention is a colored picture, a molded clay creature, a puppet show, or a play, the sense of accomplishment these achievements foster becomes obvious; indeed, often proudly exclaimed: "Look what *I* made!"

Access to the Internet and electronic publishing and design tools now provide another venue for exploration, another avenue for creative expression. Dr. Idit Harel, who holds two master's degrees from the Harvard Graduate School of Education and a Ph.D. from the MIT Media Lab, believes that using the Internet and digital media tools can help build three essential "X" skills for learning today: "eXploring, eXpressing, and eXchanging ideas." The CEO and founder of MaMaMedia Inc., a Web site for kids, Harel writes:

> "Developmental psychologists, good educators and the makers of good kids' Web sites know that constructive learning—learning that allows children to create, design or construct something of their own—empowers learners. And when learning involves the child's ideas and creativity, there is a bonus: the blossoming of self-esteem. We know that when our kids make something of their own that can be shared with others online (and offline), they feel so good about themselves that they want to go further and do more. With its almost limitless possibilities, the Web can be the perfect place for a child's creativity and

self-image to develop in a variety of important ways. Another plus is that your children are learning a vital skill for the new millennium: how to express themselves with digital media and tools. Don't worry, I am not proposing that we take away pencils, paints and building blocks. I am simply encouraging you to add a new set of tools—digital tools—that will enable your child to express herself in exciting new ways" (2000).

For an example of how libraries in New York have been presenting kids with the opportunity to use digital tools while exploring their communities, visit the Mohawk Valley Library Association's *I Spy* Web site. (www.mvla.org/ispy/). This creative project involves teams of students in grades four through eight using a digital camera to photograph historical sites in their community. Portions of the images are posted to the Web and captioned with clever rhymes that challenge the reader to guess what the snapshot depicts.

On the Web page that describes how the I Spy Web game developed, the coordinators of the project state, "New technology leads children to take a unique look at their communities in the Mohawk Valley Library Association's I Spy project. The project is making children aware of history in their own backyard, while introducing them to architecture, digital technology, and creative writing!" For a complete description of how to create your own I Spy site, visit the MVLA's "I Spy—About the Project" page, www.mvla.org/ispy/about.html.

This chapter profiles two general types of recreational programming with the Internet that librarians have initiated, providing young people with opportunities for exploration and expression:

- developing a theme Web page to feature selected sites on a specific subject for kids to explore as guided activities;
- conducting a workshop for kids to learn how to create their own Web page or electronic magazine.

I'll share some examples of how we have presented these kinds of programs for elementary-age children at Monroe County Public Library. The following libraries have contributed the other featured reports for this section:

- Martin Library in York County, Pennsylvania
  Cyber Camp Web Site and Program for School-age Students
- Ross Library, Pennsylvania
  Making a Web Page Program for Young Adults
- Monroe County Public Library, Indiana
  E-Zine Workshop for Teens

VIRTUAL DINOSAURS AND BLAST OFF! THEMED WEB SITES FOR YOUNGER ELEMENTARY

MONROE COUNTY PUBLIC LIBRARY, INDIANA

CHILDREN'S SERVICES, www.monroe.lib.in.us/childrens/childrens_dept.html

Program Title

Virtual Dinosaurs
www.monroe.lib.in.us/childrens/dinos.html
Blast Off!
www.monroe.lib.in.us/childrens/blastoff.html

Target Audience

Children in grades 1 through 3.
(*Reported by Lisa Champelli, MCPL children's librarian*)

Required Equipment

You will need Web design tools if you want to create your own Web page to use as a guide for the program. A commercial Web site, such as Kids Domain Online Dino Games (www.kidsdomain.com/games/dino.html), can also be used. Program participants need access to computers connected to the Internet and a Web browser.

The program leader may find it helpful to have a LitePro or other LCD projector to demonstrate Web navigation skills to students, but it is not essential. I have conducted this program in the library's public computing center, which can accommodate 24 participants, but the program could be done with a smaller cluster of computers. Many participants enjoy printing out pages, so a printer, although not required, is often greatly appreciated!

Program Description

When we started offering "Explore the Internet" sessions to children in grades 3 through 6, we often received requests from parents to have younger children attend. To accommodate the desires of par-

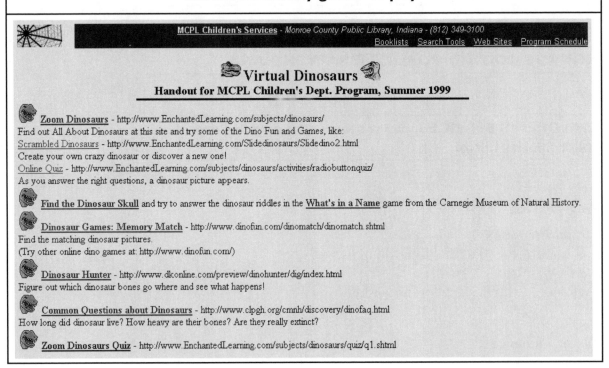

Figure 4-1: Many educational dinosaur Web sites designed for younger children include some easy games to play.

ents who wanted their children to have an introduction to the Internet, I developed a more structured program around a particular theme by preparing a Web page with preselected links to sites on the featured topic. I developed pages for two continuously popular subjects—dinosaurs and space—topics that offer myriad Web sites, many suitable for younger children.

The goals for these programs are to familiarize younger children with using a Web browser, review some tips for staying safe online, and make it as easy as possible for kids to explore Web sites on the featured topics and spend time with the interactive sections of the selected sites. Many younger children do not have the patience or reading skills required to search out sites of interest on their own. Because the themed pages are linked from the children's services Web page, under the "Web sites for Kids" heading, the children in this program can access these pages without having to type in a URL. As part of the orientation to using the browser, I demonstrate how to get to the featured page from the library's homepage.

The program is scheduled for an hour. When the participants enter the program room, the computers are usually turned on with the Web browsers already opened to the library's homepage. I have let kids start clicking on links and exploring on their own while we wait for the class to start, but I prefer to have a pencil and paper activity for the kids to do in the meantime, because some kids (and adults!) find it very difficult to end their activity when it's time to listen. Some people who have conducted computer programs with younger children suggest starting the program away from the computer entirely so that participants can listen to instructions without being distracted by the urge to push a button.

To help establish the theme for the program and visually engage the participants, I have opened this program with a CD-ROM related to the program's topic. For the *Virtual Dinosaurs* program, I demonstrated portions of Dorling Kindersly's *Dinosaur Hunter* CD-ROM, and for the *Blast Off Into Space* program, I used Dorling Kindersly's *Eyewitness Encyclopedia of Space and the Universe* CD-ROM. Known for their appealing graphics and educational content, these CD-ROMs help focus everyone's attention on the information and images I want to share with them. (The demonstration also serves to promote these items, available in our circulating collection of CD-ROMs.) Because the instructor's computer includes a CD-ROM drive and is connected to the projector, the participants can all see how I use the CD-ROM by watching the projector screen at the front of the room.

I also share some books the library has on the featured topic and make sure kids know where they can find these books in the library. Next, I introduce the Internet as another resource available in the library for finding out about something that interests you. After we review the key elements of a Web page—the scroll bar; back, home, and print buttons; the location window; and how to identify a hyperlink—we discuss some online safety tips. I demonstrate how to get to the themed program page and show one of the activities on a selected site. The participants then have the remainder of the program, from 20 to 30 minutes, for exploring the selected sites at their leisure. I try to link directly to portions of selected sites that feature games or online activities that would appeal to first through third grade and that are fairly easy to learn how to play. The main portion of this program grants participants time to try out and explore Web sites that were developed for the use and enjoyment of elementary-age children.

A few kids, no matter how many different activities are presented, will say they have tried everything in ten minutes and ask what else there is to do. I encourage kids to explore another portion of one of the selected sites. Can they find a picture of their favorite dinosaur? If they still insist they've done it all, I'll suggest they pick out a book to read until their parents return to get them. At the end of the program, I encourage everyone to check out a book to take home, along with providing a handout of selected Web sites.

Insights & Improvements

It takes two to three hours to select the featured Web sites for this program and about another hour to gather the sites I want to feature on a single, easily accessible Web page that I can readily revise and update. It's an initial investment in time to prepare a tool that I can use over and over again, and add to the children's services Web site for kids to access even outside of the program.

Although the program is intended to familiarize younger children with using a Web browser and facilitate exploration of a perennially popular topic, I have had some participants who knew how to use an Internet search tool and wanted to seek out Web sites they already knew and loved, or other topics of their own choosing. While dismayed that a few kids are not more enthusiastic about the selected topic, I am thrilled to provide them with time to learn more about their own interests, whether it's the complete list of Beanie Babies, news of professional athletes, Nintendo game secrets, pictures of their favorite pop music star, or whatever their passion happens to be at the time. Part of the value of this type of program is the feeling of ownership it instills in the children who attend and discover how the library and librarians help them investigate their own interests. Plus, no matter what they are interested in, we can review searching skills and answer questions along the way: reviewing the difference between a search engine window and the location window that displays the URL; helping to distinguish between flashy graphics and teaser ads; offering tips on finding pictures; and helping to evaluate a site's contents. Of course, the program works best with more staff to move around the room and help answer individual questions.

CYBER CAMP WEB SITE AND PROGRAM FOR SCHOOL-AGE STUDENTS

MARTIN LIBRARY IN YORK COUNTY, PENNSYLVANIA

CHILDREN'S SERVICES, www.yorklibraries.org/services/childrensvs.htm

Overview

Martin Library's Cyber Camp began in 1997 as a way to introduce technology to children. Although the premise has changed, the goal has not: to foster a love of reading and an interest in computers and technology.

For libraries that already have access to the Internet and other necessary computer equipment available to share with their patrons, providing Web-based programs is something they can do at a nominal cost. Many libraries, however, recognize that offering something new—whether it's a new service or a new program—incurs costs in some way, whether in materials or staff time. Maggie Ahrens, the children's technology trainer for Martin Library, recommends partnering with local businesses that might be interested in helping to fund programs, in addition to seeking funding from grant opportunities.

"One of the major obstacles to any program is funding," Ahrens notes. "Martin Library has actively pursued funding from a variety of sources. We approached First Union Bank and received funding for 1998, 1999, and 2000 Cyber Camps. They are so pleased with the program that they have committed to sponsoring Camp on a permanent basis. The Gates Foundation awarded Martin Library 11 computers (10 student stations and a trainer's station) and they also awarded Dillsburg Library four computers. We received funding from the School District of York City to provide summer enrichment programming and additional Camps throughout the school year. Teamwork with the community really pays off, not only in funding but in relationships, quality of service to the community, and general goodwill. A good grant writer . . . coupled with a good long-range plan can really help build the technology in your library."

Below, Ahrens describes how her library developed its Cyber Camp program.

Program Title

Cyber Camp
www.yorklibraries.org/services/cyber%20camp2000/
cyber_camp_at_ycls_libraries.htm
Cyber Camp 2001 and previous camp topics are available at www.yorklibraries.org/services/cyber%20camp2000/
Cyber%20Camp.htm.

Target Audience

Children between the ages of 8 and 13
(*Reported by Maggie Ahrens, the children's technology trainer for Martin Library, in collaboration with Lora-Lynn Stevens*)

Figure 4-2: York County Libraries' *Cyber Camps* combine computer and craft time.

Cyber Camp at YCLS Libraries

sponsored by FIRST UNION

In conjunction with Summer Reading Club 2000
"Masters of the Millennium"

Explore Technology at Martin Library!

for educators

Text document about the program   Power Point about the Program

Two years ago, Martin Library's staff began the Cyber Camp program to complement and highlight the Summer Reading Club program. Since its inception, the program has undergone a number of changes but has managed to stay true to its purpose; to foster a love of reading, and an interest in computers and technology.

The sites remain available to children long after the "guided tour" of cyberspace is over. We feel that they are ideal as sources for reports, science projects, home schooling, or for general information.

All sites have been thoroughly researched and are deemed suitable for children.

Required Equipment

Computers with access to the Internet and a Web browser; craft materials. Martin Library has conducted *Cyber Camp* in the summer once a week, with two sessions on the same day. With a ten-computer lab we could seat 20 kids per week. Over the seven-week session, we could conceivably reach 140 kids.

Of course, that's not exactly how it happened. We actually filled 135 seats (kids were sick at the last second, parents forgot, and so on) with 64 different kids. Although many of the kids only attended one session, several returned for three, five, or even (in the case of one enterprising child) six sessions. The average was two sessions per child. To be fair, we allowed signups four days ahead of time. Each week, the 20 spaces for signups were filled up *within 1 hour* of the library's opening. The six additional slots on the waiting lists were routinely full as well.

The sessions last two hours and are broken up midway by a craft, which takes about 20 to 30 minutes to do. This allows the kids to get up and stretch, and also allows them to fashion a souvenir of their "voyage" that frequently serves as a further teaching aid.

In October 2000, Martin Library also started offering *Virtual Voyages* programs (www.yorklibraries.org/services/Childrens/Virtual%20Voyages/Virtual%20Voyages.htm) for two hours on Thursday evenings twice a month.

Figure 4-3: Each week of *Cyber Camp* presents children with new Web sites to explore and a new craft to create (www.yorklibraries.org/services/cyber%20camp2000/cybercamp2000.htm).

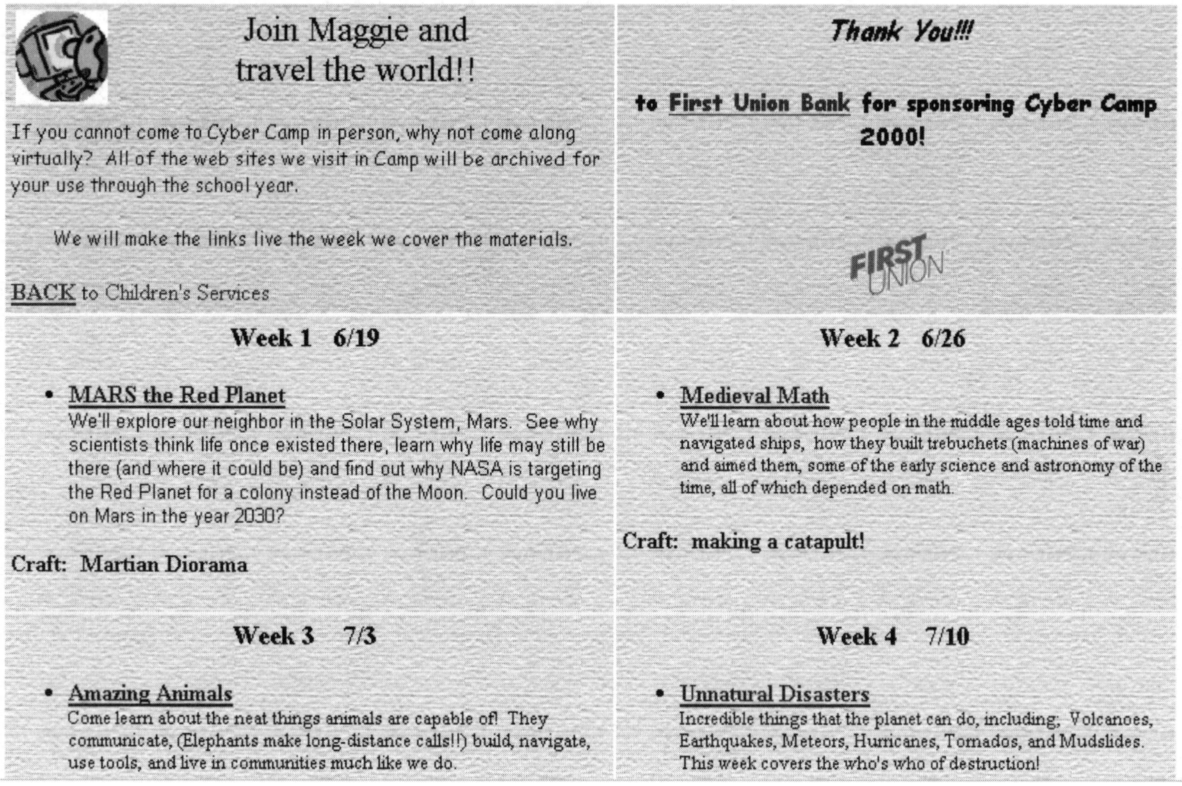

Join Maggie and travel the world!!

If you cannot come to Cyber Camp in person, why not come along virtually? All of the web sites we visit in Camp will be archived for your use through the school year.

We will make the links live the week we cover the materials.

BACK to Children's Services

Week 1 6/19

- **MARS the Red Planet**
  We'll explore our neighbor in the Solar System, Mars. See why scientists think life once existed there, learn why life may still be there (and where it could be) and find out why NASA is targeting the Red Planet for a colony instead of the Moon. Could you live on Mars in the year 2030?

Craft: Martian Diorama

Week 3 7/3

- **Amazing Animals**
  Come learn about the neat things animals are capable of! They communicate, (Elephants make long-distance calls!!) build, navigate, use tools, and live in communities much like we do.

Thank You!!!

to First Union Bank for sponsoring Cyber Camp 2000!

Week 2 6/26

- **Medieval Math**
  We'll learn about how people in the middle ages told time and navigated ships, how they built trebuchets (machines of war) and aimed them, some of the early science and astronomy of the time, all of which depended on math.

Craft: making a catapult!

Week 4 7/10

- **Unnatural Disasters**
  Incredible things that the planet can do, including; Volcanoes, Earthquakes, Meteors, Hurricanes, Tornados, and Mudslides. This week covers the who's who of destruction!

Program Description

Strictly speaking, this is a themed learning unit. In plain speech, it is a two-hour "guided tour" of the Internet. The children sign up for a session that has a theme (example: Things That Are Older Than Your Parents) and they have some idea of what we will cover, such as dinosaurs, Ice Age animals, and mummies. The trainer leads the kids from Web page to Web page, pointing out areas of interest, asking questions, getting the kids to read out loud to each other, and generally performing as a teacher would.

This type of program is a way to get kids interested in technology. It is a means of breaking the "Marian the Librarian" stereotype. It gets kids and parents calling the library and stopping by, and gives reluctant readers a positive taste of the library, which may lead to a book-loving adult.

Many children view the Internet as one big playground. Many adults view the Internet as one big sewer. Both perceptions are in-

---

Figure 4-4: *Cyber Camp* leaders share both informative facts and fun activities found online (www.yorklibraries.org/services/cyber%20camp2000/MARS.htm).

Thank You!!!

to **FIRST UNION®** *for sponsoring*

Cyber Camp 2000!
Cyber Camp Home

For centuries people have wondered what it would be like to live on another planet. We are now at a time where that is not only possible, but is being planned for by the scientists at NASA. Could we have a colony of people on Mars? Yes! Not only that, but if it happens in the year 2030, **you'll** be the perfect age to go.

Fun Stuff

- space fun
- play and do
- M&M astronauts
- Make your own Alien

How We're Getting There

- Mars Academy Goals
- Gathering information for the mission
- Missions in Space...past and future

The people with the Plan

- MARS Exploration at NASA
- The Planetary Society

---

correct, and we can use *Cyber Camp* to show both parties that the Internet can be fun, educational, safe, and exciting.

We are also helping bridge the "digital divide." Children who have no access to computers at home know that they can come into the library and use "their" computers. They go to school just as prepared to learn as their classmates. Technology is no great mystery to them because they went to "camp" over the summer.

If you're hosting a Cyber Camp that someone else has created, preparation involves a few things: the time and energy to familiarize yourself with the materials, four or more Internet-ready computers, and the staff and the energy level to host the camp. You also need to pull books that are pertinent, and place them close to the camp area or by checkout. Materials for crafts are optional, but a very good idea. You can use less expensive materials than those we have listed, which some of the libraries in York have chosen to do.

If you're building the site, preparation involves everything for hosting a Cyber Camp and a few additional important components. You need to select suitable Web pages and Internet sites. Link them to a library Web page (using HTML code or a Web page editor), and make sure that they are interesting, educational, and have no inappropriate material. Select a craft that reinforces the theme; the craft is made halfway through the camp to alleviate wandering interests or fidgety kids.

If you choose to build your own site, be aware that the Web has certain limitations. For example, Martha Graham was a great modern dancer, but there is little (realistically) you can do with that on the Internet. A better choice would be animals. Not only is there greater interest, but there are many sites out there that have interactive learning, Shockwave games, educational sites, print and play toys, and great pictures. Things that move, react, or make noise hold children's interest well.

Some people have a romp with technology, really like children, and pick up new computer skills with the greatest of ease. If you have someone like that on your staff, you have the ideal person for Cyber Camp.

If instead you have someone who loves children, and you have a different person who is good at computers, and a third person (a reference librarian, for example) who is good at finding Web sites, then you have a team that will allow you to make a great Cyber Camp. The important thing to remember is that these people all need to sit down and *communicate*. Be very specific with each other in what you want the topic to be, using as many descriptive words as you can.

Below is a sample dialog: T=trainer, or the person who is going to be working with the kids. R=researcher, or the person who is finding the Web sites. W=Web person, or the person who is building the page with the sites provided by the researcher.

T: "I want to teach kids about animals—jungle animals, not farm or domestic animals."
R: "Jungle as in Africa, or jungle as in South America?"
W: "Do you want a jungle print around the page? How about moving animals on the main page?"
T: "Um . . . the print looks good, and I think South America sounds good—close to home."
R: "So we can include animals from South America. How about people and culture? Do you want me to include animals that live in zoos but are originally from South America? The National Zoo has a great Web cam so the kids can see the animals live!"
W: "And how do you want this organized on the page? I can link it from our front page so the kids can see it right away from home, or I can put it on our resources page."
T: "Well, the zoo idea sounds good, but no personal pages of pets that are wild animals. I think that's a bad idea. As far as organization goes, I like your idea about the front page for now, then we can move it to the resources page after the camp is over. It'll function as advertising for the camp on the front page"

Trainer Notes

For use with CyberCamp 2000, Week 5 Session

Things That Are Older Than Your Parents

http://www.yorklibraries.org/services/cyber%20camp2000/cybercamp2000.htm

The following outline describes what to cover and how to refer to the Web sites used in each session.

Dinosaurs

- *Dino Timeline: gives the kids a chance to see the different ages of the Dinosaurs*
- *Meat Eaters*
  - o *5-10 min* Sue the T Rex *info on the famous t rex skeleton*
  - o *2-5 min* Image of T Rex *(used this as a discussion of camouflage)*
  - o *2-5 min* Extinction of the T Rex. . . *did a meteor really cause the extinction of Dinosaurs? (yes. . . they think the crater is off the coast of Mexico)*
  - o *2-5 min* Deinonychus *related to Raptors. . . discuss the things that make it a good hunter (camouflage, binocular vision, teeth and claws)*
  - o *2-5 min* Mega Raptor *very big raptor, and probably ran in packs, too*
  - o *Jurassic Park Stills from the Movie*
- *5-10 min Plant Eaters*
  - o *Jobaria*
  - o *Micro Ceratops (not all dinos were huge!)*
  - o *Apatosaur*

Compare the meat-eaters to the plant-eaters, and discuss the differences (binocular vision vs wide-view vision, packs vs herd behavior, possible parenting skills and styles). To help the kids visualize, try comparing a fox to a rabbit, or a wolf to a deer.

- *Different Dinos*
  - o *Alphabetical List*
  - o *National Geographic*
  - o *Dinosaur Hall*
  - o *Dinosaur Eggs*
  - o *Assortment of Dinosaurs*
  - o *Many Dinosaur Links*
- *Other Stuff*
  - o *5-10 min* ROACHES! *Good for some fun. The Roach existed before dinos did, and is still alive today. Discuss why.*
- *Neat Facts*
  - o *Walking with Dinosaurs*
  - o *How did they know that?*

o *They were not alone*
o *Mama Ovaraptor*
- *Why the Dinosaurs became extinct (good for discussion. . .)*

Old Sea Critters

- *2-8 min* Savage Ancient Seas *(if it works, you can look out a porthole and see the sea)*
- *1-2 min* Colacanth *thought to be extinct, this fish appears in the fossil record, but was caught and has been seen today!*
- *2-4 min* Ichthyosaur *ask the kids what they think that this critter may look like (dolphin and shark) and what it may have eaten (fish). Form follows function!*
- *3-5 min* Critters from the Cretaceous *look and see. . . some of these critters are still around today (turtle, diving birds, nautilus)*

Ice Age

Ice Age Land Critters
Most of these pictures will offer the kids a chance to see how big, odd, and unusual the animals of 10,000 years ago were. Unlike dinosaurs, mankind lived at the same time as these creatures. A few topics to discuss with the kids would be:
How could people protect themselves from big predators? What weapons did people of this time have? How did people of the Ice Age live?
- *1-2 min Bison (still around today)*
- *3-5 min Saber Toothed Cats. . . what do they most resemble? (Lion) What were the teeth for? (Probably to bring down prey)*
  o *Sketch (Great Picture)*
  o *Photo (not as great)*
  o *Fossil (re-assembled skeleton)*
- *3-5 min Giant Sloth they're extinct, but relatives (3 toes) are still around*
  o *skeleton*
  o *Mount*
- *1-2 min Cave Bear*
- *1-2 min Really Odd Critter (looks like a rhino, but knobby. . . I don't know what the knobs are for, but you can ask the kids what they think)*
- *1-2 min a tundra critter*
- *3-5 min a list of critters that **survived** the Ice Age*

Mummies

- *5-10 min* Mummies 101 *a good overview of mummies*
  o *In a nutshell, there are 3 kinds of mummies*
    - *Dry mummies (desiccated by heat)*
    - *Cold dry mummies (ice=freezerburn)*
    - *Pickled mummies (tannic acid in the bogs)*
  o *Compare to drying flowers or making pickles. . .*

- *up to 20 min all other mummies (choose what you find to be most interesting)*
- *5-10 min* Animal Mummies *(all 3) People mummified their pets,(cats and antelope) live-stock (bulls) and sacred animals (Ibis and Crocs). Really neat stuff!*

Other sections of the Web site for this program include:

- Fun and Games
- Parents and Educators - *The contents of this area are full of worthwhile activities that take too many resources or too much time for me to include them in Cyber Camp. If I thought to myself* "Gee, that's neat!! I really wish I could do that for Cyber Camp. Too bad!" *it got placed here*
- Photo Gallery - *is a selection of different prints and fossils that didn't really fit anywhere, but worked as a useful resource for kids with homework, reports, or curiosity.*

When you build, consider the source of the Web pages. Pages will vary greatly in usability. A poor example would be "Sherri Berry Dino Land" where you can "adopt" a virtual dinosaur. That might be cute, but it is of no practical use to you. Other sites, such as www.discovery.com or www.nationalgeographic.com or maybe the Smithsonian's Web page, are great resources and have a wide variety of useful and educational (as well as fun) activities. Use a little logic; if it's a major magazine, educational television show, or organization, it probably has a Web site. Some personal pages may be of worth, but do a little research and make sure there's no direct link to an inappropriate Web site.

Insights & Improvements

Most of the cost of this program is incurred in staff time. Hosting one session of the camp with 20 children in attendance required eight hours of the trainer's time (three hours to review and learn material, four hours of actual teaching time, and one hour for setup/teardown) at $10 per hour. Craft materials cost $24.42, for a total of $104.42 or $5.22 per child.

If you choose to build a class yourself, estimate $13\frac{1}{2}$ hours of the trainer's time (seven hours to find sites and build the page, $1\frac{1}{2}$ hours to get craft materials, four hours of actual teaching time, and one hour for setup/teardown). Calculating trainer time at $10 per hour and allowing $25 for craft materials brings the total to $160, or $8 per child (for 20 students). Although more expensive, this allows you to customize the class to suit your program.

Don't think that you can't host the camp just because you have a small budget. The second year of Cyber Camp we had no budget to speak of; the crafts ranged from paper tube rockets to print-and-color pages. The most important thing you can do for the program is to have a pro-child, pro-technology person in place *who likes to have fun*. At Martin one year, with no budget, we built paper rockets, went up a flight of stairs, and launched them into the main reading room. We glued tongue depressors to clothespins and shot split peas from our "medieval catapults." A child's imagination and enthusiasm only need a little encouragement.

If you went to a local business (or your board of directors) and asked for more than $200 to teach 20 children about dinosaurs, I don't think you'd get very far. However, if you justify the expenses as a means to reach the kids, possibly get good press, add a resource to your Web site, and join a growing community of technology-savvy libraries, it might go over a little easier. Spreadsheets are an easy way to track spending and clearly explain what you're going to spend the money on.

When people read in the paper or see on the news a library full of happy excited children it changes their thinking. If, in the article or broadcast, they hear one or more people gush about how the camp keeps their kids stimulated and active over the summer, it could also change their attitude, perception, and maybe their vote for library funding. In a nutshell, this is a great opportunity for your library and your community. You can increase circulation and keep kids reading and learning over the summer. You can incorporate this into the summer reading club program as we have, or use it as a stand-alone. Most importantly, we can share the efforts of individual libraries and combine them into something really impressive.

Cyber Camp can have an enormous impact on your library, the children you teach, and the community as a whole. It helps shake the misconception that we are nothing more than a dusty book warehouse. It defeats the belief that libraries are static, unexciting places, and that librarians cherish quiet over all other things. We are grabbing the future and running with it, and that is all to the good!

Contact Person

Maggie Ahrens, Youth Technology Specialist
York County Library System
(717) 846-5300, ext. 234.
mahrens@yorklibraries.org

WEB DESIGN WORKSHOP

MONROE COUNTY PUBLIC LIBRARY, INDIANA

CHILDREN'S SERVICES, www.monroe.lib.in.us/childrens/ childrens_dept.html

Overview

Realizing that the Web is the medium of their children's era, parents of children who have attended Web design workshops conducted at Monroe County Public Library have expressed their gratitude for the library sponsoring this type of program and have encouraged continued sessions. But the time it takes to learn about some of these new tools and prepare a program to teach children and young adults how to use them earns its reward tenfold from the delighted expressions of the kids themselves, thrilled to see what they have created.

Program Title

Web Design Workshop
www.monroe.lib.in.us/~lchampel/webprogintro.html

Target Audience

Children in grades 3 through 6
(Reported by Lisa Champelli, MCPL Children's Library)

Required Equipment

Computers with access to Internet and a Web browser; Notepad, Wordpad, or other simple text editing program; and formatted $3\frac{1}{2}$-inch disks. I have conducted this program in the library's public computing center as one-and-a-half-hour sessions on three consecutive days. The center can accommodate 24 participants, but you could certainly do this program with a smaller cluster of computers. I find it very helpful to use a LitePro projector to demonstrate viewing the source code for a Web page and to display my example coding for kids to refer to as they create their own pages. Even though I distribute handouts to kids with the example codes on it, some find it

---

Figure 4-5: You'll find many HTML tutorials online, but creating your own allows you to tailor your instruction to the structure of your program.

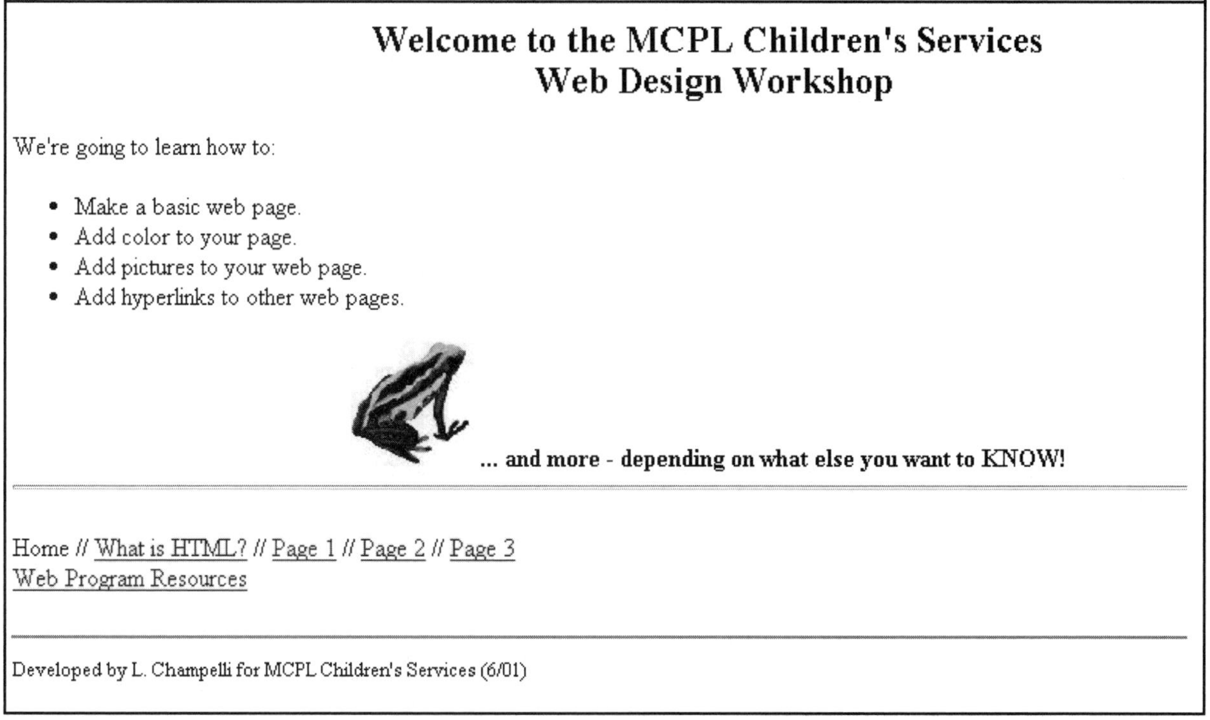

Welcome to the MCPL Children's Services Web Design Workshop

We're going to learn how to:

- Make a basic web page.
- Add color to your page.
- Add pictures to your web page.
- Add hyperlinks to other web pages.

... and more - depending on what else you want to KNOW!

Home // What is HTML? // Page 1 // Page 2 // Page 3
Web Program Resources

Developed by L. Champelli for MCPL Children's Services (6/01)

---

easier to refer to the screen for the latest code we're writing. You could use transparencies and an overhead projector to the same effect.

Program Description

When the kids first enter the computing center, I give them each a disk and ask them to write their name on it, letting them know that this disk is theirs to keep. I usually give them a word find or crossword puzzle to do while we're waiting for everyone to arrive.

The main goal of this program is for children to learn enough basic HTML code to be able to create their own simple Web pages. We learn how to make text larger and smaller, how to add color to a page, how to find and save free clip art images, and how to link to another site. I explain to the kids that although they will be creating Web pages and viewing them with a Web browser, their pages won't actually be on the World Wide Web. I explain: For your page to be added to the Web, it needs to go and live on a Web server computer. For this workshop, your page will live on your disk.

THE FIRST DAY

I give an overview of what the workshop will cover. We talk a little bit about what the Internet is and what the World Wide Web is. We talk about how anyone can make a Web page and put it on the World Wide Web, and I let them know that they can create their pages about anything that they would like—as long as it's something they wouldn't mind having their mom or dad see. I make sure everyone is comfortable using the Web browser, and that they know how to use the scroll bar and other tools.

We then start looking at the individual codes needed to make a Web page. I show the class the Web page I made for the workshop and I demonstrate how to view the source code by going to the View menu bar in Netscape and selecting "Page Source." I explain that the codes tell the Web browser to make the text look a certain way. I explain that some codes have a partner, and some codes can stand alone, but every code has to be written between angle brackets (< >) to keep the code invisible.

Next, I open Notepad and begin typing the standard codes that every Web page has to have. I type just a few sentences and then demonstrate how to save text as an HTML file to the disk, by making sure to give the filename an .html ending. I point out to kids that the first time they save their file, they "Save As" but after they add to it, they should just choose "Save." (Otherwise, some kids "Save As" every time. They end up with multiple files with slightly different names, and it's hard for them to keep track of which one is their latest version.)

Next we view their file through the Web browser to see what they look like! (To do this, choose "File" from the browser menu, select "Open Page," and click on "Choose File," and direct the browser to look in the A drive.) I distribute handouts with the instructions for how to do what I just demonstrated, and the kids start writing their own pages as I (and as many assistants as I can recruit) walk around the room to help and to answer questions. By the end of the first session, the kids should have been able to view their files through the Web browser and have their beginning Web pages saved to their disk. The kids who "get it" quickly start adding more text and trying out the different codes to get the text to appear larger, smaller, in bold, and so on. At the end of the session, I collect their disks for safekeeping until the next session.

SECOND DAY

I review how to open the saved .html file in Notepad in order to add to it. We quickly review what we learned in the first session, then I demonstrate how to change the background color of the page and how to change the font color. I show them a Web site listed on the resource page (www.monroe.lib.in.us/~lchampel/webprogres.html) that they can use for finding the specific color codes to use in Web pages. Then I return the children's disks and they have about 20 minutes to play around with the color options.

When I'm sure that each child has had a chance to add some color to his or her page, I ask for everyone's attention again so that we can learn how to add a picture to the page. First, I introduce the issue of copyright and explain that usually when someone creates a story or picture, they own it and they get to decide if and how anyone else can use it. The picture and clip art sites I refer kids to have all given permission for others to use the artwork for free on personal homepages, but some ask that a credit line appear on the page featuring the artwork. So I encourage kids to check a site for permission information to make sure they have the right to copy and use images from another Web page. (See *Clip Art Collections—Images for Your Web Page*, www.monroe.lib.in.us/~lchampel/imgarch.html.)

Invariably, kids want to copy images from commercial sites, whether it's the Nintendo, Lego, or Barbie homepage. I caution them against doing this, advising that most companies are very concerned about the images they own because they want to be sure everyone knows which is the official company homepage. Because I know the temptation will be too great for some kids, I insist that if they use images from a company Web site, they *must* acknowledge where the image came from.

Then I demonstrate how to copy an image and save it to my disk by moving the mouse arrow over the image and clicking the right mouse button. When the menu window pops up, I choose "Save Image As," give the image an easy name to remember, take note as to whether it's a .gif or .jpg, and tell the computer to save it to the A drive. When the image is saved to disk, I go back and open the .html file in Notepad and insert the image on the page using the <IMG SRC="imagename.gif"> code. After saving the file, we view it through the Web browser and *voila*! Kids have the remainder of the session to search for and add images to their pages. At the end of the session, they again leave their disks with me.

THIRD DAY

I return the children's disks as they arrive, and they are free to work on their pages while we're waiting for the others. I ask if anyone has any questions about what we've done so far. In this session we learn how to add hyperlinks to their pages so that they can link to another page.

First we discuss how to use search tools. Some kids have the impression they can get to anything by guessing a URL or typing keywords into the location window. This is an opportunity to teach some more effective ways of finding information on the Web. I tell them they can find a link to selected Internet search tools from the Program Resources page. I use Yahooligans to demonstrate searching for a topic of popular interest. I show them how to highlight and copy the URL and paste it directly into a file so they don't have to write down addresses and type them into the code. The kids then have the rest of the session to search for sites they might want to link to, or to add more text or pictures of their choosing. Some kids even create second and third pages so they can link their own pages to each other.

At the end of this session, I give kids the option of leaving their disks with me if they would like me to add their pages to the Monroe County Public Library's Web site for a while so that their pages will be part of the World Wide Web. Only a few kids have taken me up on this offer. Nearly all prefer to take the disk home with them. Apparently, the disk in hand provides more real, tangible proof of ownership.

Insights & Improvements

I recently tried conducting this workshop as a single three-hour session. Every child managed to create a page with some color and a picture on it, but it was much too frantically paced. The program assistants and I spent much more time trying to fill in the gaps in areas that I didn't have time to cover as part of the group instruction. I didn't have time to discuss search tools, and I encountered several kids who had no idea how to navigate down through a subject directory even after I had connected them to a starting point. While the goal of this program is to create a Web page, it also serves as a way to discuss copyrights and the importance of citing sources, and to introduce some search tools or techniques that kids might not be familiar with.

I also have found that kids learn a lot from each other. They lean over to the person sitting next to them to share suggestions and admire a cool image they found. They get up to see what their friend across the room has made. It's an exciting, collaborative process! When parents ask if they can stay for the program, I explain that they may observe from the back if they like, but the program is intended for kids, some of whom are more inhibited when a parent is in the room.

Next, I'd like to develop a program for parents and children to create a Web page together and learn how to have it live on the World Wide Web.

Contact Person

Lisa Champelli, Children's Librarian
Monroe County Public Library
303 East Kirkwood Avenue
Bloomington, IN 47408
lchampel@monroe.lib.in.us

MAKING A WEB PAGE PROGRAM FOR YOUNG ADULTS

ROSS LIBRARY, PENNSYLVANIA

www.rosslibrary.org/

Overview

I teach kids how to do HTML markup "from scratch" partly because it gives kids an additional sense of control to understand what it is that makes the page look a certain way, and partly because that's the way I first learned so it's the method I know best. But it's hardly the only way to go about it!

Pam Henley, a technical assistant responsible for maintaining Bozeman (Montana) Public Library's Web pages, conducted a Web design program for teens while she was the young adult librarian. Henley explains that although teens used the library, the librarians hadn't focused on programming for teens as a way to get them to the library more often. She offered the *Design Your Own Web Page* program as an activity that would attract teens.

Henley borrowed ten laptop computers that her state library loans. Running on battery power for the class (held in the library's meeting room), the laptops can all access the Internet and include Netscape Composer, a Web page editor that comes with the freely available Netscape Communicator Web browser. The first time she offered the program, it was structured as a three-day class (two hours each day), but the second time she held it for two days (still two hours each day) and felt that timeframe worked fine too.

The program begins with a brief discussion of good Web page design. "We keep this brief," Henley says, "because they are just dying to get their hands on the laptops! We go to Composer and begin demonstrating the different aspects."

Henley finds that creating Web pages is an activity that is best done individually, although friends might be able to work cooperatively to make a Web page. She initially offered the program to middle-school students, ages 12 to 15. "The second time we offered the program to high school students, ages 14 to 18, and felt this worked much better. The first (younger) group needed a lot of individual attention," Henley recalled, "but the older group just took off and really got creative."

Denise Selmar-Larsen, young adult librarian for the Ross Library in Pennsylvania, opened up her *Web Design Class* to young adults ages 12 to 18. She describes her program below.

Program Title

Web Design Class

Target Audience

Young adults, ages 12 to 18
(*Reported by Denise Selmer-Larsen, young adult librarian at
Ross Library in Lock Haven, Pennsylvania*)

Required Equipment

Computers with a Web browser and access to the Internet. We use the Web page editing tools at the Tripod Web site (www.tripod.com) to create the Web pages. We have eight computers available to us in the main part of our library, so classes are limited to eight people. We do not use any projectors.

Program Description

I decided to do this program because I wanted something that would encourage teens to read! They love computers, so what better way to lure them? Read a book, design a Web page describing the book.

My flyers describing the program said, "Spin a Web at the Ross Library." There was a spider web and a brief description of the class: "Read a book and design a Web page . . ." The teens choose a book to read in advance of the program and design a Web page describing the book, using text and pictures that they import from the Net.

To prepare for this program, I advertise in the local paper and hang flyers around the library and in the schools. I do a lot of gabbing with the kids when they come in too! The day before the program, I place signs near the computers and at the main desk warning the public that the computers will not be available during the class time (very important here at Ross, as we have a lot of computer traffic).

Our computers are in groups of four, all in the same room in close proximity to each other. They all have Internet access and the catalog on them, but we have two computers at the main desk if patrons need to look at the catalog while the class is going on.

The classes themselves are two hours long and meet three times for a total of six hours, usually enough time to design a page. The kids make their Web pages with Tripod (www.tripod.com), which offers easy and advanced versions. I evaluated other Web building sites on the Net, but Tripod was the one I liked best.

I tell the kids to go to www.tripod.com and I explain that this is a Web page building site. The teens pick their own user name and password to start using the site. It only takes a few moments to sign up. I have them read Tripod's directions and tell them to ask me if they need any help. Of course, I am working with ages 12 to 18, so they know a lot already, but the site is very easy to understand.

At the beginning of the class I hand out lists of clip art sites, .gifs, and other images, and most of the kids know where to go to get the pictures that they need. During the program I am simply there to offer assistance if needed.

Insights & Improvements

I will continue running this program in the summer. All the librarians here at Ross are very supportive of the program! It brings a lot of activity into the library and all patrons seem to enjoy the hub commotion. Patrons wander over and check it out.

The young adults can teach you so much. All you need to do is listen. I have enjoyed watching how they help each other, give each other ideas for their pages, and are willing to share. I am very fortunate to be able to work with a great group of teens.

Contact Person

Denise D. Selmer-Larsen, Young Adult Librarian
Ross Library
232 West Main Street
Lock Haven, PA 17745
(570) 748-3321

E-ZINE WORKSHOP FOR TEENS

MONROE COUNTY PUBLIC LIBRARY, INDIANA

TEEN SERVICES, www.monroe.lib.in.us/teens/index.html

Overview

Dana Burton, teen services librarian for the Monroe County Public Library, wanted to provide local teens with an opportunity to express themselves on the Web in whatever creative style they chose. But the Web Committee for MCPL has established style guidelines for pages that are part of the library's Web site. In order to give teens freedom to control the Web design of their teen magazine, *E-zine* has its own Web site, hosted by a local nonprofit community network and Internet service provider. In the following report, Dana describes her goals for the program, and how the teens put the magazine together.

Program Title

E-zine
www.bloomington.in.us/~e-zine

Target Audience

Middle school and high school students, ages 13 to 18
(*Reported by Dana Burton, teen services librarian*)

Required Equipment

One computer with Internet access and a room or office in which to meet are basic needs, but having several more computers available is great. A projector for displaying computer screens on the wall is a nice extra so that more people can view the screen at once. A digital camera and a scanner are also helpful if you want to include original artwork in the e-zine. If a digital camera is used, plan to have access to a paint program and a photo editor program.

We have held meetings in a library program room with tables, chairs, and access to a computer with an Internet connection and an easy-to-use Web editor such as Netscape Composer.

Figure 4-6: For three consecutive years, Monroe County teens have produced their own Web-based magazine.

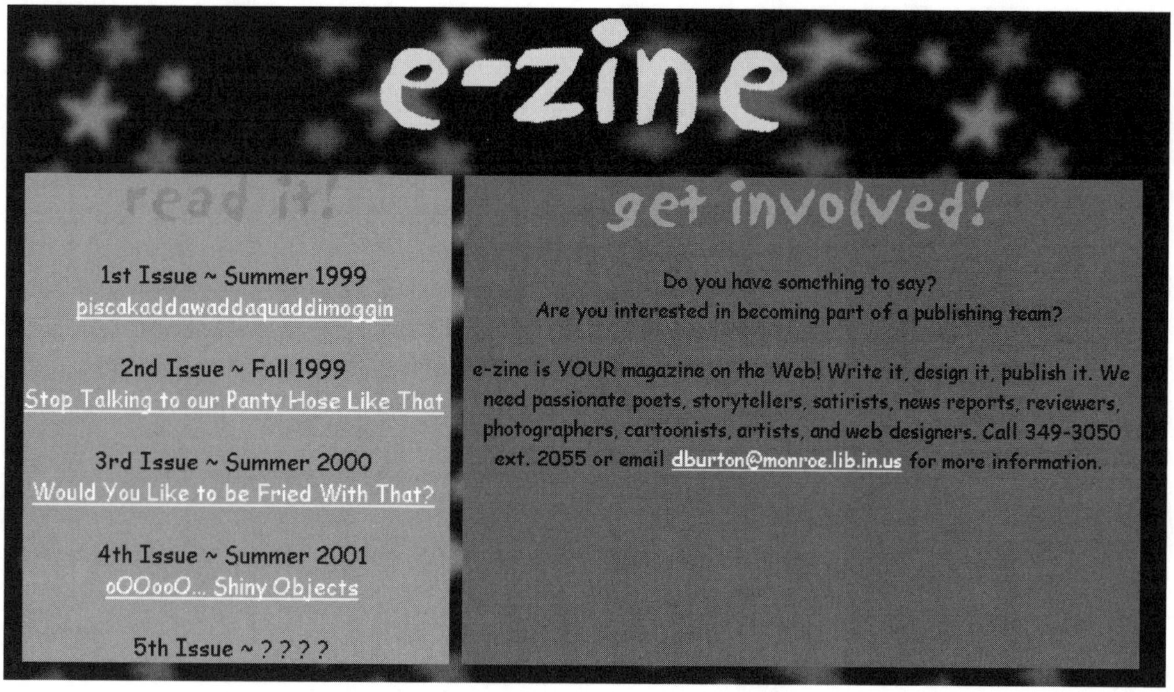

Program Description

E-zine is an electronic magazine published by teens for teens. The library's teen services sponsors a program that facilitates the opportunity for teen writers, artists, and Web designers to create an edition of *E-zine*. Three editions have been produced. Each group names, organizes, designs, and contributes writing and art for their edition. The group is asked to work out editorial policies as well as content, layout, and design.

Publicity for the programs runs along these lines:

E-zine—it all started with *Piscakaddawaddaquaddimoggin*, starring teen writers from the Bloomington area. Interested in contributing? Check out the site for more info. www.bloomington.in.us/~e-zine *E-zine* is YOUR magazine on the Web! Write it, design it, publish it. We need passionate poets, storytellers, satirists, news reporters, reviewers, photographers, cartoonists, artists, and Web designers.

1st Issue—Summer 1999
Piscakaddawaddaquaddimoggin

Figure 4-7: Teens get to control the content for their unique publication (www.bloomington.in.us/~e-zine/would/home.html).

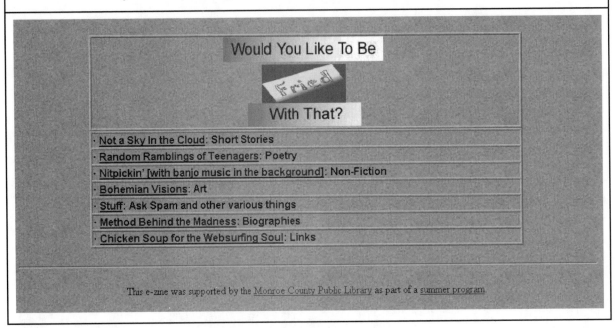

2nd Issue—Fall 1999
Stop Talking to our Panty Hose Like That
3rd Issue—Summer 2000
Would You Like to Be Fried with That?

E-zine fits a variety of goals. Process and product are equally important. It is educational; it encourages teens to explore literature and the arts on a personal level as well as develop writing skills and explore editorial and publishing issues. It is recreational in that it is offered as a leisure-time activity, not a "learning experience." And it is an important part of our role as teen advocate: *E-zine* was created to highlight the literary and artistic talents of local teens, to provide a venue for featuring the talents and skills that teens already have to offer the community. It fits the library's and teen services' goals to "facilitate informal education of all people in the community, and to provide encouragement and support for self-development, creative expression, and communication by people of all ages" (library goal #1), "act as an advocate for teens within the library and community" (teen services goal), and "provide windows to the future: create programs and services that introduce teens to skills and technology that they may need or use as adults" (teen services goal).

The first meeting involves decisions regarding categories for content, creating a time line, working out a name, dividing the work. Later meetings begin with a group meeting and then time to work individually or in groups. After the first meeting, Web designers spend time creating a front page, contents, credits, and a template for pages. Near the end, the group is asked to move from writers and artists into an editorial board. At some meetings, all work is read aloud and everyone is encouraged to talk about what they like about each piece. Editorial policies, free speech, censorship, group versus individual ownership of the magazine, and many other issues will come up throughout the work sessions—there might be some great discussions! The last meeting is a revealing of the final magazine, a time of celebration and food!

As one of the guidelines we establish for the program, we insist the teens only use first names or pseudonyms to protect their identities, especially since the Web address we're using for the e-zine is so obviously geographic. Because the magazine is primarily a local publication, the teens receive the individual recognition they deserve from their peers and the local community; word gets around as to the real names of the artists and writers. The use of first names and pseudonyms provides some protection and yet allows them an audience outside of their hometown.

The first issue of *E-zine* was conducted with a young adult intern who knew HTML and shared her knowledge with the teens who didn't already know how to make a Web page. But many of the teens already know HTML. For the other issues, the designers used Netscape Composer, which is pretty easy to use.

Teaching HTML was not on our agenda. We figured that if teens already had experience using a Web editor, they could transfer any experience with one Web editor to another. Besides being relatively easy to use, we decided to use Netscape Composer because it is available in our own library's public computing center. As the team worked at the library, we knew we could reserve several computers in the computing center at any time during the program. Those who learned to use it could come back anytime and use it for their own purposes for other Web projects. In all cases, the intern worked out glitches and did the final posting of the Web page to the free account space provided by a local Internet service provider.

Insights & Improvements

E-zine has been offered as a summer program and as an after-school program. The best schedule may be two- to three-hour meetings every day for one to one-and-a-half weeks. Energy and interest lagged when we met once or even twice a week. Therefore, summer might be the best time to offer this program.

If you have the expertise to facilitate group work with teens but not the technical skills for Web design, find a community volunteer or partner. A college or high school technical assistant can offer troubleshooting advice and will be a great addition to the team. Be sure to include this person in the planning from the very start!

Everyone is sensitive about the value of his or her own work. Unless asked for help, it is best to let writers edit and proofread their own work. It is important to set up a safe, comfortable session in which to read, share, and praise everyone's efforts. Although it is initially hard for some to let others read their work, doing so often creates a sensitive and satisfying sharing session. Few will eagerly agree to this session, but it might be the only time team members will hear good things about their work. It's empowering, important, and worth doing.

Contact Person

Dana Burton, Teen Services Manager
Monroe County Public Library
303 East Kirkwood Avenue
Bloomington, IN 47408
www.monroe.lib.in.us/teens
dburton@monroe.lib.in.us

Chapter 5

The Youth Cybrarian's Source Box

Use of the Internet by young people has received more than its share of negative press. I hope the reports featured in this book depict some of the positive, innovative ways librarians are using the Internet with young people to help develop their information literacy skills and powers of creative expression. As different as the programs are, they share a common element: collaboration. Nearly all of the librarians who have shared information here report collaborating with colleagues, whether it's on the development of content for the program, selecting featured Web sites, or determining the graphic images that will define a Web page. Talk with your library's Web administrator (or others with Web design skills) about what you'd like to do. Solicit the advice and skills of volunteers and interns who can help you create what you envision.

Give yourself time to design a new program, but don't expect perfection the first time you present it. Evaluate your audience's response and make adjustments as you discover what works and what doesn't. Take along your sense of adventure, your joy for discovery, and, of course, have fun!

The Internet and rules for governing its use continue to evolve at such a rapid pace that it's difficult to predict what the online environment for young people will look like in the next year, much less the next decade. Web portal sites for kids that blossomed in 1997 have already gone bust. Legislation for regulating Internet content and services continues to be proposed and rejected or adopted in various stages and forms. New Web search and design tools emerge all the time.

Perhaps as today's generation grows up with the Internet and incorporates it into their daily lives, tomorrow's parents will be more confident instructors and facilitators of their children's online activities. Even so, I expect youth librarians will continue to play a role in educating children about the best practices for using the Internet and participating in online communities in a smart and safe manner. Certainly, youth librarians will continue to teach school-age students how best to search out information on the Web and evaluate Web resources to enhance their research. And I anticipate they will continue to encourage children to explore recreational interests through engaging online resources, and provide opportunities for young adults to express themselves and convey their creativity with digital tools. The following resource lists are included here to help you stay informed and continue to learn more.

INTERNET SAFETY TIPS AND TUTORIALS

Safety Advice

Child Safety on the Information Highway
www.safekids.com/child_safety.htm
Written by Larry J. Magid for the National Center for Missing and Exploited Children, puts the risks of Internet use in perspective. Suggests guidelines for parents. See also www.safekids.com/safeteens/safeteens.htm.

Children's Partnership—Parent's Guide to the Information Superhighway
www.childrenspartnership.org/bbar/pbpg.html
Straightforward background information and advice for families.

Cybersavvy—What Should I Do If . . .?
www.cybersavvy.org/cybersavvy/parents/1b3.html
The Direct Marketing Association suggests role-playing some online risk scenarios with children so they will be prepared to respond wisely.

GetNetWise—Online Safety Guide
www.getnetwise.org/safetyguide/
Safety tips for kids, teens, and parents. Suggests safe use guidelines for various ages.

Librarian's Guide to Cyberspace for Parents and Kids
www.ala.org/parentspage/greatsites/safe.html
From the American Library Association; provides direct, clear advice.

PBS Kids—Get Your Web License
www.pbskids.org/did_you_know/license/
Learn the rules of the road and get an official Web license when you pass the test.

Safe Surfin'
www.safesurfin.com/index.htm
Find some safety tips, great sites, and take the Drivers Ed Challenge.

World Kids Network—Internet Safety
www.worldkids.net/school/safety/internet/internet.htm
Includes chat and e-mail safety and courtesy tips.

Tutorials for Learning about the Internet

Learn the Net—Getting Started
www.learnthenet.com/english/html/00start.html
Provides clear explanations and appealing graphics.

WebTeacher Tutorial—Your Source for Web Knowledge
www.webteacher.org/winexp/indextc.html
Comprehensive tutorial developed for K-12 instructors.

Examples from Public Libaries

Baltimore County Public Library, Maryland, *The Internet and the World Wide Web*
www.bcplonline.org/kidspage/tutorial.html
Attractive tutorial explains how to navigate the Web and use a search engine.

Boston Public Library, Massachusetts, *About the Internet: Kids' Page*
www.bpl.org/kids/AboutInternet.htm
Includes an Internet dictionary, Netiquette tips, and advice for using the Internet with school reports.

Burlington County Library, New Jersey, *Internet for Kids*
www.burlco.lib.nj.us/Classes/Intforkids/
Very clever tutorial covers how to use the mouse, scroll, and identify links before explaining what the Internet is and how to search the Web.

Delaware County Library System, Maryland, *The Internet and You: A Parent's Guide*
www.delco.lib.pa.us/pweb.html
Includes tips and resources for parents, and recommended sites for kids too.

London Public Library, Canada, *Internet Safety—What You Need to Know!*
http://discover.lpl.london.on.ca/static/generic/90
Includes tips for kids and parents, information for parents, and an Internet safety quiz for kids.

Minneapolis Public Library, Minnesota, *Web for Kids*
www.mpls.lib.mn.us/webforkids.asp
Features an Internet safety quiz with artwork by illustrator Lane Smith.

San Jose Public Library, California, *My Rules for Internet Safety—KidsPlace*
www.sjpl.lib.ca.us/Kids/isafety.htm
Advice to children and tips for parents.

Waterford Township Public Library, Michigan, *Kids—Internet Tutorial*
www.waterford.lib.mi.us/children/jnettutorial.htm
Clearly composed tutorial includes section on Internet safety.

SEARCH TOOLS

The art and science of locating just the information you need from an Internet site is an ever evolving practice. Many of the search tools designed to scan and select sources to match your query change as regularly as the seasonal decorations in department stores. Just when you think you've got one figured out, it adds a feature, alters its structure, or merges with another Web site (or in some cases, disappears altogether).

The search tools highlighted here have proven to be reliable ones to use with school-age children. (The term "search tool" here refers to both search engines and subject directories.) There are many others out there, and often it's necessary to use a general search tool to help a student answer a homework question. The journal articles and Web sites listed in the "Articles and Web Sites About Search Tools and Strategies for Searching the Web" reference section of this list will help you learn more about the different search tools available, decide which ones to use when, and how to discuss their differences with the children and young adults you teach.

Search Tools for Kids

KidsClick!
http://sunsite.berkeley.edu/KidsClick!/
A superior, ad-free search tool designed for kids by a group of librarians at the Ramapo Catskill Library System in New York. Browse the directory listings, use the keyword dialogue box, or try the advanced search option. Each resource included in *KidsClick!* is annotated and includes a notation about illustrations, reading level, and a subject heading. Kids who aren't sure how to spell a word but know what letter it starts with can access the list of subject headings with the alphabetical index. You can also choose to view the directory "through a Librarian's eyes," which transforms the subject headings listed in the directory into Dewey decimal number categories.

The Ramapo Catskill Library System (RCLS) librarians also developed guided lessons to teach different methods for searching the Web (see: www.worldsofsearching.org/index.html). These lessons refer to other search tools for kids, but the homepage for *KidsClick!* also includes direct links to RCLS's collections of other useful search tools, such as *Image Search Tools* (www.kidsclick.org/psearch.html), good for finding pictures of things ranging from art to animals, history to space; *Sound Search Tools* (www.kidsclick.org/ssearch.html), good for finding songs and other audio files on the Web; and *Kid's Search Tools* (www.kidsclick.org/ksearch.html), which lists other search tools designed for kids, such as *Ask Jeeves for Kids* (www.ajkids.com/). This collection also includes other online research tools kids might want to use to support their search for information on the Web, including dictionaries and encyclopedias.

Yahooligans!
www.yahooligans.com/
Although included with RCLS's list of kids' search tools, *Yahooligans!* is a tool you might choose to start with when you're helping kids search for information or pictures of pop-culture topics. For example, the *KidsClick!* database includes one site for Britney Spears. *Yahooligans!* has 45 sites and subcategories for "Britney Spears—pictures," "Britney Spears—videos," and "Britney Spears—sounds."

Other Search Options and Guides for Children

The Ramapo Catskill Librarians are careful to point out in one of their Search Lesson pages that search tools for kids do not block access to any Internet resource. The database that these tools use are small, carefully selected collections of sites reviewed by a human being who has decided that the content is appropriate for children, but the search tool does not prevent anyone from using the browser to visit other sites on the Web. Because the collection of sites is relatively small compared to the databases of other search tools, some libraries have started linking to general search tools that provide an option to have their collection of sites filtered to exclude pages that might be inappropriate for children.

Search Tools with Filters
www.monroe.lib.in.us/childrens/searchfilter.html
The Children's Services Search Tools page for Monroe County Public Library includes links to search tools designed for children, a couple of general search tools, and a link to a page of search tools that includes options for conducting a search with the "search guard" or "family filter" on to screen out results that would be unsuitable for children. While no filter is 100 percent effective, these tools give young people the option of searching a larger database with more confidence that their results list will not include objectionable language or images.

Other Web sites that include listings of various search tools for kids include:

TekMom's Search Tools for Students
www.tekmom.com/search/

Oswego City School District's page of Children's Search Engines
www.oswego.org/ocsd-web/teaching/kidsearch/kidssearch.htm

The following Web sites for kids are a few of the ones that emphasize help with homework:

CyberSleuthKids—An Internet Search Guide for the K–12 Student
http://cybersleuth-kids.com/

FactMonster—From Information Please
www.factmonster.com/

Homework Center—Homework Topics
www.multnomah.lib.or.us/lib/homework/
Selected by Multnomah County Library, Oregon.

Homework Help—Student Resources
www.kcls.org/hh/homework.html
Selected by King County Library System in Washington

Web Portals for Kids

A Web portal is a Web site with a collection of tools or services targeted to a certain audience. The site collects and designs resources that encourage visitors to remain at the site or return on a regular basis. There are a number of Web portals designed for kids. They generally include games kids will enjoy as well as information resources geared to children. Some provide children with the ability to create their own homepages, take part in chats, or obtain a free e-mail account.

Alfy
www.alfy.com/
Geared to early elementary-age children.

Bonus.com
www.bonus.com/
Content for elementary-age children and older

Headbone Zone
www.headbone.com/
Designed for children ages 8 to 14.

Kiddonet
www.kiddonet.com/
A place for children ages 3 to 12 to play, create, and communicate online.

MaMaMedia.com
www.mamamedia.com/
Designed for children 12 and younger.

Zeeks.com
www.zeeks.com/
Geared to kids ages 6 to 13.

Note: There is an array of Web portal sites for teens, but many of these seem especially designed to market products to teens. For a general listing of teen sites, see Google's Web directory listing for *Kids and Teens: Teen Life: Web Communities* (http://directory.google.com/Top/Kids_and_Teens/Teen_Life/Web_Communities/).

Articles and Web Sites about Web Search Tools and Strategies

Back to the Wall: Have Search Tools for Students Improved?
www.slj.com/articles/chatroom/20010201_9507.asp
In the February 2001 issue of *School Library Journal*, Walter Minkel evaluates four popular search tools students might use to find information for a homework report.

Choose the Best Search Engine for Your Need
http://nuevaschool.org/~debbie/library/research/adviceengine.html
The curriculum coordinator for Nueva School in California, Librarian Debbie Abilock lists sample information needs and suggests the best search tool and strategy for locating the information. This site includes a link to an animated tutorial about using Web search tools.

Finding Information on the Internet: A Tutorial
www.lib.berkeley.edu/TeachingLib/Guides/Internet/FindInfo.html
This comprehensive tutorial developed by the Teaching Library at the University of California, Berkeley, recommends search strategies, describes different types of search tools, presents a table comparing the best search engines, suggests ways for evaluating search results, provides a glossary, and more!

Kathy Schrock's Guide for Educators: Critical Evaluation Surveys
www.school.discovery.com/schrockguide/eval.html
Provides forms for students to use (one each for elementary, middle, and secondary school grade levels) to help them analyze Web sites they consult for school projects. Includes related articles Schrock has authored and links to articles others have written about evaluating Web sites.

The InvisibleWeb: The Search Engine of Search Engines
www.invisibleweb.com/
A directory listing more than 10,000 specialized databases, archives, and online resources for targeting the source of needed information.

Search Engine Guide
www.searchengineguide.com/
A knowledge base of search engines, portals, and directories established by industry experts.

Search Engine Watch
www.searchenginewatch.com/
Created by an Internet consultant and journalist, this site reviews and rates search engines, provides tips for Web searching, and reports related search engine news. Includes a listing of kids' search tools (www.searchenginewatch.com/links/Kids_Search_Engines/).

SearchIQ
www.zdnet.com/searchiq/
ZDNet, a Web site for people looking to buy, use, and learn more about technology, reviews and recommends search tools. Also spotlights a daily search tip and links to search tutorials and guides.

Smith, C. Brian. "Getting to Know the Invisible Web: How to Get at the Internet's Hidden Resources." 2001. *NetConnect* supplement to *Library Journal* and *School Library Journal*. (Summer): 16–18.
Describes online information that is inaccessible via general search tools, and tells how to reach the content contained in specialized databases.

Web Search Engine FAQS: Questions, Answers and Issues
www.infotoday.com/searcher/oct01/price.htm
Gary Price, a research and Internet consultant, aims to answer recurring questions about Web search tools in the October 2001 issue of *Searcher* magazine, a publication for professional database searchers. The insightful article lists ten things to know about five popular search tools, the limitations of general search tools, and the development of new Web search tools.

WEB DESIGN TOOLS

There are a gazillion places to go on the Web to learn about HTML and how to design Web pages. The following sites are aimed at teaching children and young adults these skills. Most of these instructional sites include their own suggestions for finding clip art and places to host your page, so take time to explore their recommendations in addition to the ones listed here.

HTML/Web Design Tutorials

Learning HTML
www.ipl.org/youth/kidsweb/
The Internet Public Library Youth Division explains what HTML is,

defines different tags, discusses copyright, and includes links to more Web page design resources.

Learning HTML for Kids
www.goodellgroup.com/tutorial/
In 12 clear chapters, the author of this tutorial starts by explaining basic concepts and finishes with creating tables. Also includes two points for pausing to review.

Lissa Explains It All: HTML Help for Kids
www.lissaexplains.com/intro.shtml
Covers the basics as well as more advanced skills, such as creating frames and adding JavaScript to pages. Also includes a great list of useful tools.

Web Diner's Web Adventure
www.webdiner.com/webadv/index.htm
Offers beginning, intermediate, and advanced tutorials, as well as templates. Clearly organized to help you build your page in stages.

WebGenies—Web Design for Kids
www.webgenies.co.uk/index.htm
Provides lessons, projects, resources, and information on Web careers for children ages 5 and up. Includes tips for parents and teachers on how best to structure lessons to teach children at various age levels.

Webmonkey for Kids
www.hotwired.lycos.com/webmonkey/kids/
Includes lessons to follow, tools to use, and a planning guide for parents and teachers.

Free Clip Art Sites

Animation Factory
www.animfactory.com/
A collection of images that move. Includes a few images in each subject area, such as animals, children, creatures, school, and many more.

Awesome Clipart for Kids
www.awesomeclipartforkids.com/
Offers a general subject index and a holiday index with categories of free family-friendly images. Includes a "School Zone" category and an index to puzzles and worksheets you can create online.

IconBAZARR
www.iconbazaar.com/
Provides both icons and images in a number of different categories ranging from critters to food, presidents to stars. Topic headings indicate whether the category includes any animated images. Also includes listing of color tables for learning designated codes for adding color to Web pages.

Kid's Domain Clip Art Index
www.kidsdomain.com/clip/
Extensive index to icons and clip art organized by popular subjects, such as animals, space, holidays, seasons, and more. Includes links to a number of other clip art sites offering graphics with children's themes.

Free Web Page Hosting Sites

The following sites provide a sampling of places on the Web where you can create and post your own Web page. These host sites are free in that you don't have to pay them a fee to house your Web page, but you are required to carry their advertisements on your personal Web page. You'll want to read the terms of service to learn about the special tools and rules each site has. See *Lissa Explains It All: Free Web Hosts* (www.lissaexplains.com/hosts.shtml) for a listing of some lesser-known hosting services that do not require you to carry ads on your page.

Angelfire
http://angelfire.lycos.com/
Owned by Lycos, provides tools for beginner, intermediate, and advanced Web builders. Allows users to customize banner ads to some degree.

The Express Page
http://expage.com/
Simple Web page construction. Free, but includes banner advertisements.

Tripod
www.tripod.lycos.com/
Also owned by Lycos, provides various Web building tools for different skills levels. Users can choose which type of ad (pop-up or banner at top of page) appears on their pages. Tripod also offers an online environment exclusively for teachers and students at http://classroom.tripod.com/.

Webspawner
www.webspawner.com/
Can create very simple, basic Web page for free, but obligated to include banner or pop-up ad. Does permit transfer of .gif and .jpg files from your computer to the Web page.

Yahoo Geocities
http://geocities.yahoo.com/home
Have the Pagewizards create the page for you or use the drag and drop Pagebuilder HTML editor to create your own.

HTML and Web Page Editors

Software that can help you write HTML and create Web pages.

Arachnophilia
www.arachnoid.com/arachnophilia/index.html
This HTML editor is available for free as careware. Includes tutorials for HTML, JavaScript, and more. Download the full or smaller version from the Web for use on your own computer.

BBEdit Lite
www.barebones.com/products/bbedit_lite.html
This free text editor with HTML capabilities is designed for use with Macintosh computers only. Download from the Web for use on your own computer.

SNS HTMLEdit
www.snsware.com/htmledit/
Another free HTML editor. Download this program from the Web to use on your computer.

HTMLEdit
www.jimtools.com/htmledit/
If your Web browser can handle JavaScript and dynamic HTML (the author of the program suggests either the Netscape Communicator 4 or Internet Explorer 4 Web browser), you can run this program via your Web browser. No downloading required.

Macromedia Dreamweaver
www.macromedia.com/software/dreamweaver/
Highly recommended Web site design and management program. Dreamweaver Web site includes tutorials for learning how to use the software. Version 4 costs $299. You can download a free 30-day trial program.

Microsoft FrontPage
www.microsoft.com/frontpage/
A Web site creation and management program. Web site for FrontPage includes tutorials for learning to use the software. Price for new users listed at $169. You can order a 30-day trial program on CD for $9.95.

Graphic Design Tools

Adobe Photoshop
www.adobe.com/products/photoshop/main.html
Professional image editing software. Tutorials and other customer support are available online. Version 6.0 cost $609. You can download a free tryout version; however, tryout product does not permit you to save, export, or print any artwork.

Photoshop Elements
www.adobe.com/products/photoshopel/main.html
An easier-to-use version of Photoshop, available for $99. A free 30-day tryout version also is available.

Macromedia Fireworks
www.macromedia.com/software/fireworks/
Create, edit, and animate Web graphics. Samples and tutorials for learning to use the software are available from the Web site. Version 4 costs $299. You can download a free 30-day trial.

Paint Shop Pro
www.jasc.com/products/psp/
Graphics design software. Tutorials available on the Web site. Version 7 cost $99. Free 30-day trial version also is available.

WEBSITE MANAGEMENT TOOLS

Link Checking Software

These tools make sure all the hyperlinks in your Web page connect to the linked site without errors.

Link Valet
http://valet.htmlhelp.com/link.html

W3C Link Checker
http://validator.w3.org/checklink

HTML Validation Tools

These tools make sure that your HTML code is correct. Some also check links.

Doctor HTML
www2.imagiware.com/RxHTML/

HTML Tidy
www.w3.org/People/Raggett/tidy/

W3C HTML Validation Service
http://validator.w3.org/

Web Design Group—HTML Validator
www.htmlhelp.com/tools/validator/

Additional Web Development Reference Sources:

The following sites are chock-full of useful tools and answers to your questions about how to make the Web work for you!

CNET.com—The Source for Computers and Technology
www.cnet.com/

Library Web Manager's Reference Center
http://sunsite.berkeley.edu/Web4Lib/RefCenter/

Web Developers Virtual Library—Encyclopedia of Web Design Tutorials, Articles and Discussions
www.wdvl.com/

Webmonkey—The Web Developer's Resource
www.hotwired.lycos.com/webmonkey/

WebReference.com—The WebMaster's Reference Library
www.webreference.com/

Website Tips
http://www.websitetips.com/

INTERNET FILTERS AND OTHER INTELLECTUAL FREEDOM ISSUES

The libraries featured in this book have varying methods for managing use of the Internet. Some use blocking and filtering tools; some do not. All have policies describing the library's rules and guidelines for using the Internet in the library. Many of these policies are posted to each library's Web site. Whether you need to develop a policy for Internet use, especially by children and teens, or defend your library's position on this matter, you can consult the online resources prepared by the American Library Association. The following sites offer a wealth of educational information and recommended policies regarding filtering and recommended practices for providing Internet access to the public.

Filters and Filtering
www.ala.org/alaorg/oif/filtersandfiltering.html
Index of the American Library Association's Policies and Statements on Filtering and of sites that provide further information on filtering, especially in regards to children and their parents, and much more. Compiled by the Office of Intellectual Freedom.

The Internet—Especially for Children and Their Parents
www.ala.org/alaorg/oif/children.html
An index to online resources addressing use of the Internet by children and teens.

Libraries, Children and the Internet
www.ala.org/parents/librariesandinternet.html
Lists common questions and answers regarding use of the Internet by young people in libraries.

Libraries, the Internet and Filtering Fact Sheet
www.ala.org/alaorg/oif/librariesfact.html
Briefly describes how filters work, cites studies reporting the effectiveness of filters and other news reports about Internet use, and explains the role the American Library Association takes in helping libraries manage public Internet access.

Reports on Internet Filters

The Cyber-Library: Legal and Policy Issues Facing Public Libraries in the High-Tech Era
www.ncac.org/issues/cyberlibrary.html

Very thorough article outlines the ways libraries are using the Internet to serve their communities and the impact that attempts to censor Internet access in public libraries have on First Amendment freedoms.

"Digital Chaperones for Kids: Which Internet Filters Protect the Best? Which Get in the Way?" 2001. *Consumer Reports* (March): 20–23.
Explains how filters work and which ones are the most effective.

Identifying What Is Harmful or Inappropriate for Minors
www.ncac.org/issues/minors.html
The National Coalition Against Censorship's *White Paper* submitted to the Committee on Tools and Strategies for Protecting Kids From Pornography attempts to assess any harm caused to minors exposed to pornography and other inappropriate Internet content. Issued March 2001.

Internet Filters: A Public Policy Report
www.ncac.org/issues/internetfilters.html
The Free Expression Policy Project of the National Coalition Against Censorship surveyed all studies and tests it could find describing the actual operation of 19 products or software programs commonly used to filter Web sites and other Internet communications. This report, released Fall 2001, summarizes the results of that survey.

Filtered or Unfiltered?
www.slj.com/articles/articles/20010101_9371.asp
Article by Professors Ann Curry and Ken Haycock for *School Library Journal* (January 2001) summarizes results of a survey to determine how many school and public libraries have filtering software and the level of satisfaction with the various brands used.

FilterGate, or Knowing What We're Walling In or Walling Out
www.infotoday.com/MMSchools/may01/wolinsky.htm
Article by Art Wolinsky for the May/June 2001 issue of *Multimedia Schools* examines how filters end up blocking some sites erroneously.

GetNetWise
www.getnetwise.org/
Coalition of corporations and public interest organizations joined to produce this detailed Web site to help families make informed deci-

sions about using the Internet. Resources include an "Online Safety Guide," a listing of tools for guiding, regulating, or monitoring use of the Internet, information on how to report problems to legal authorities, suggested Web sites for kids.

Maxwell, Nancy Kalikow. "Alternatives to Filters." 2001. *American Library Association TechSource: Library Technology Reports* (March-April): 1–60.
Extremely thorough analysis of how filters work and other methods libraries have for managing public Internet access. Includes an estimated cost of each method.

Safeguarding the Wired Schoolhouse
www.safewiredschools.org/publications.html
The Consortium for School Networking (CoSN) designed this site to help school leaders understand their technological options for managing the content students access over the Internet. Materials include a detailed briefing paper and a summary available as a PowerPoint presentation, a "Checklist for Decision-Making," and a listing of other online resources.

Privacy Issues

COPPA: The Children's Online Privacy Protection Act
www.ala.org/oitp/privacy.html
The American Library Association's Office for Information Technology Policy explains how this federal law impacts children, parents, and librarians.

Kidz Privacy
www.ftc.gov/bcp/conline/edcams/kidzprivacy/index.html
Web site developed by the Federal Trade Commission helps children, teachers, and other adults understand online privacy laws and issues.

Privacy Resources for Librarians, Library Users and Families
www.ala.org/alaorg/oif/privacyresources.html
Provides index to policies developed by the American Library Association and other online sources that help educate the public and professionals about privacy issues.

Organizations Promoting Intellectual Freedom Issues

American Civil Liberties Union
www.aclu.org/

American Library Association's Office for Intellectual Freedom
www.ala.org/alaorg/oif/

Center for Democracy and Technology
www.cdt.org/

Electronic Frontier Foundation
www.eff.org/

Free Expression Network
www.freeexpression.org/

WEBQUESTS AND EDUCATION PORTAL WEB SITES

Where do you go for online assistance when you're looking for Web-based lesson plans, recommendations of good Web sites to use with students, and other suggestions for integrating technology into the classroom or a library program? There are many such sources to choose from, available for free on the Web, and even more subscription services.

The resources listed here include a sampling of some Web portal sites for educators, Web sites for learning about WebQuests, and some innovative educational Web sites to use with students.

Web Portals for Educators

A to Z Teacher Stuff: PreK–12 Network
www.atozteacherstuff.com/
Created for teachers by a teacher, the site features online lesson plans organized by themes, subjects, and grade level, and searchable by keyword. Also includes printable resources, articles, tips, and chat for teachers.

Awesome Library: K–12 Education Directory
www.awesomelibrary.org
Organizes selected Web resources by subject. Includes categories for teachers and librarians, as well as kids, teens, and parents. Site is searchable by keyword.

Bigchalk.com: The Education Network
www.bigchalk.com/
Offers both subscription-based educational products and free tools for students, teachers, and parents. Categorizes best Web resources for study and research, lesson plans, students, parents, teachers, library/media specialists, and administrators. Provides ability to search for best sites on the Web by grade level.

DiscoverySchool.com
www.school.discovery.com
Provides innovative teaching materials for teachers, useful resources for students, and advice for parents about how to help their kids enjoy learning. The site is reviewed for educational relevance by practicing classroom teachers in elementary school, middle school, and high school. Tools include clip art gallery, puzzle maker, worksheet generator, lesson plans, encyclopedia, dictionary, and more.

Education World: The Educator's Best Friend
www.education-world.com/
Aims to make it easy for teachers to integrate the Internet into the classroom. Includes a search engine for educational Web sites only. Search for or browse topics in the database of more than 500,000 Web resources. Or search for useful information in a particular section of "Education World": article archives, subject resources, specialties, or the reference center.

Gateway to Educational Materials
www.thegateway.org/
The National Library of Education (NLE) and the U.S. Department of Education collaborated to create this one-stop educational resource. Sites listed provide information, lesson plans, and activities pertaining to all K–12 subjects. Users can browse sites by subject or keyword, or they can search by subject, keyword, title, or full-text of the site description.

Kathy Schrock's Guide for Educators
www.school.discovery.com/schrockguide/
Terrific categorized list of sites useful for enhancing curriculum and professional growth. Updated often to include the best sites for teaching and learning. Includes sections on Internet information, search tools, critical evaluation, and WebQuests.

WebQuests and Other Ways to Teach with the Web

FOCUS: Five Rules for Writing a Great WebQuest
www.iste.org/L&L/archive/vol28/no8/featuredarticle/dodge/index.html
In the May 2001 issue of *Learning and Leading with Technology*, published by ISTE, the International Society for Technology in Education, Professor Bernie Dodge shares his tips for creating high-quality WebQuests. Includes links to references and related online resources.

TeAch-nology Tutorials: Using the Internet to Stimulate Higher Order Thinking: Enter the WebQuest
www.teach-nology.com/tutorials/web_quests/
Reviews the reasons for conducting a WebQuest, describes how to make your own WebQuest (without learning how to make a Web page) and provides an index to hundreds of WebQuests found on the Web, organized by subject. This site also functions as an "Educational Portal," containing links to lesson plans, terrific teacher tools, worksheets and worksheet makers, and other online tutorials.

WWW4Teachers: The Online Space for Teachers Integrating Technology into the Curriculum
www.4teachers.org/
Features acceptable-use policies, explanations and examples of WebQuests, organized by subject, and tools for developing Web-based learning projects. Developed by the High Plains Regional Technology in Education Consortium.

The WebQuest Page
http://edweb.sdsu.edu/webquest/webquest.html
Developed by Bernie Dodge, a Professor of Educational Technology at San Diego State University, this site gives an overview of what a WebQuest is, selected examples by subject and grade level, training materials for developing a WebQuest and learning more about them, and tools for communicating with other WebQuest developers.

Wired Learning: Web-Based Lessons, Activities and More!
www.kn.pacbell.com/wired/wired.html
Pacific Bell's Knowledge Network Explorer includes a wealth of online materials created by an application design team of former teachers and librarians. The site includes sample WebQuests, the "Blue Web'n" library of online learning applications, and tools for creating Web pages and posting them to the Web.

Innovative Educational Sites to use with Students

BrainPOP
www.brainpop.com/
Produces animated movies about health, science, and technology concepts in a visually entertaining and educational style. Featured subjects correspond to the National Science Education Standards for grades 5 through 8. Each subject contains a three- to four-minute animated movie, an interactive quiz, an experiment, a comic strip, a how-to hands-on application, a time line, and a printable activity page.

Eduweb: Educational Web Adventures
www.eduweb.com/adventure.html
Immersive, interactive, and in-depth adventures about art, science, and history. Eduweb specializes in developing educational games, simulations, and learning modules to bring educational content to life. Topics range from "Leonardo's Workshop" to "Tracking the Tiger Trade."

The Exploratorium: The Musem of Science, Art and Human Perception
www.exploratorium.com/
Visit the Learning Studio for a monthly index of cool educational sites and fascinating online and interactive exhibits on a range of topics from the brain to frogs. Visit the sport science section for online features profiling the science involved in baseball, mountain biking, skateboarding, hockey, and other sports.

Franklin Institute Online
www.fi.edu/
Discover how to incorporate online museum exhibits into lesson plans. Visit the learning resources section of this site for a number of online activities that promote inquiry and critical thinking. Discover science activities, puzzles, educational hot lists, and more.

FunBrain.com
www.funbrain.com
Find free educational games for preschool and school-age children. Search for games by age, subject (math, history, language arts, science, music, geography, art, technology, and physical education), title, or keyword. Descriptions of each game are included in the curriculum guide section for teachers. For a subscription fee, teachers can also create customized quizzes.

NASA Kids
http://kids.msfc.nasa.gov/
Provides a fun way for children ages 5 to 14 to learn about NASA's activities and science using interactive tools and attractive pages. Includes online or printable resources and related curriculum materials for teachers. Visit NASA's other sites for children: *NASA's Space Place* (http://spaceplace.jpl.nasa.gov/spacepl.htm) and *NASA Space Shuttle Virtual Tour* (http://science.ksc.nasa.gov/shuttle/missions/sts–90/vrtour/frame2.html).

The Odyssey: World Trek for Service and Education
www.worldtrek.org/odyssey/info/index.html
Aims to promote global awareness among youth. Students track the activities of a team of educators as they travel to featured locations and post reports of their journey. Students can also interact with the team via chats, e-mail, polls, and discussion boards. Complementary lesson plans, based on National Education Standards, can be used in conjunction with the trek or separately.

ThinkQuest
www.thinkquest.org/
This nonprofit organization offers programs designed to advance education through the use of technology. The Web site lists resources for creating Web pages, and the ThinkQuest Library of Entries, a collection of more than 4,500 educational Web sites designed by participants in the ThinkQuest competitions. The competitions motivate students and educators to work collaboratively in teams to create Web-based learning materials that teach others. Teachers and learners can explore a multitude of educational topics by browsing the list of entries, using the search tool, or browsing previous winners.

Virtual Field Trips
www.field-guides.com/
Provides a means to present information on science and nature and other topics as a guided and narrated tour of Web sites that have been selected by educators and arranged in a "thread" that students can follow from site to site with just the click of a single button. Each annotated field trip lists teacher resources required for the trips. Web site also includes information on the software used to create the online field trip.

The Why Files
whyfiles.org/index.html
Supported by the National Institute of Science Education at the Uni-

versity of Wisconsin, Madison, this site uses news and current events as springboards to explore science, health, environment, and technology. The engaging, timely stories are classified according to National Science Education standards for grades 5 through 8 and 9 through 12. Browse topics by subject or theme, or search the site archives.

LIST OF PROFESSIONAL ASSOCIATION WEB SITES AND LISTSERVS FOR YOUTH LIBRARIANS

Many librarians serving children and teens in schools and public libraries work without the benefit of in-house or local peer support. Professional associations and online discussion groups can help you communicate and consult with other youth service librarians.

Professional Associations

American Association of School Librarians (AASL)
www.ala.org/aasl/

Association for Library Service to Children (ALSC)
www.ala.org/alsc/

Young Adult Library Services Association (YALSA)
www.ala.org/yalsa/

Listservs/Online Discussion Groups

YALSA Mailing Lists and Web Sites
www.ala.org/yalsa/professional/yalsalists.html

LM_NET School Library Media Specialists
http://ericir.syr.edu/lm_net

PUBYAC, Children and Young Adult Services in Public Libraries
www.pallasinc.com/pubyac

WWWEDU, The World Wide Web in Education List
www.ibiblio.org/edweb/wwwedu.html

Web Sites for Practicing Librarians

ICONnect
www.ala.org/ICONN/
Supports school library media specialists as they assume leadership positions in the use of the Internet in the school community.

Librarians' Index to the Internet
www.lii.org/search
A searchable, annotated subject directory of more than 8,300 Internet resources selected and evaluated by librarians for their usefulness to users of public libraries.

Libraries for the Future
www.lff.org/
Nonprofit organization dedicated to helping libraries achieve their historical mission in an interactive environment.

Peter Milbury's Network of School Librarian Web Pages
www.school-libraries.net/
Links to pages created by school librarians and helpful resources.

School Libraries on the Web
www.sldirectory.com/
A directory of Web pages maintained by K–12 school libraries.

Young Adult Librarian's Help/Home Page
http://yahelp.suffolk.lib.ny.us/
Created by librarian Patrick Jones, this site compiles resources of interest to YA librarians, ranging from a sampling of Web sites for teens to YA literature.

Glossary

Adobe Acrobat. A type of software developed by Adobe that enables documents created in one format to be displayed and printed on another platform in exactly the same way. Acrobat documents are called PDF (Portable Document Format) files. Details available: www.adobe.com/products/acrobat/.

Browser. The computer software used to display information on the Web. Two common Web browsers are Netscape and Internet Explorer.

Chat. A way of communicating via the Internet by typing messages to one or many people at once in real time. Sometimes special software is required, but many Web-based chat sites are easily available. Chat sites usually ask users to register or log in with a screen name. Chat sites for children are often monitored, sometimes via an automated program that blocks forbidden words, or sometimes via a human supervisor who makes sure the messages comply with the rules for that chat site.

Cyber. A prefix that indicates relationship with the world of computers, especially the Internet. *Cybrarian* refers to a librarian who is comfortable using Internet tools.

E-mail. Electronic mail. A way of sending messages electronically from one computer to another. E-mail can include attachments of images or other kinds of files.

GIF. Graphics Interchange Format. A file format for saving color graphics. GIF files, often used in Web pages, end with the .gif file extension.

HTML. HyperText Markup Language. The written code used for creating hypertext documents, or Web pages. HTML code (or tags) contain formatting commands a Web browser interprets to display the text and graphics of the HTML document in a certain way. HTML documents can be named with either the .htm or .html file extension. (HTML standards are developed and maintained by the World Wide Web consortium. See www.w3.org/.

HTML Editor. A program that inserts HTML codes into a document.

HTTP. HyperText Transfer Protocol. The protocol or set of standard rules used to transmit and receive data via the World Wide Web. When you type a URL beginning with "http" into a Web browser, you initiate a request for a Web server to return information to your computer using HTTP.

Hyperlink. The code embedded in a document that enables you to jump from one portion of the document to another, or from one page to another. Hyperlinks in Web pages most often include the URL specifying where to locate a certain Web page. Links usually appear as underlined or highlighted text, or text of a different color. Graphic buttons or images can also be used to indicate a hyperlink.

Hypertext. Text that includes links, which enable you to jump from one section or page to another.

Internet. A global network of computers that can communicate with each other using a common language called TCP/IP (Transmission Control Protocol/Internet Protocol).

Java. A programming language developed by Sun Microsystems that adds animation and other action to Web pages. Some Web browsers are automatically configured to run the small Java applications called applets.

JavaScript. A written code that can be added to standard HTML pages to create interactive documents.

JPEG. Joint Photographic Experts Group. Another format for image files used in Web pages. JPEG files can contain millions of colors (as opposed to GIFs, which are limited to 256 colors), but this format can compress the image better than the GIF format, which makes the files smaller and faster to download. JPEG filenames end with the .jpg file extension.

LCD. Liquid Crystal Display. LCD refers to the way that the image gets projected onto a screen, but people often use this as shorthand to refer to the projector they are using to display a computer screen to an audience. The *HowStuffWorks* Web site explains: "Most laptop displays or monitors incorporate LCD, while a desktop display or monitor uses a CRT (cathode ray tube) to output text and graphics images." Details available: www.howstuffworks.com/monitor1.htm.

Listserv. Software for managing and distributing e-mail messages submitted by users subscribed to an online discussion group. The name also is used now as a synonym for online discussion group.

Plug-in. Refers to software designed to be used in conjunction with a larger application, such as a Web browser. Web browsers can be designed to accept special plug-ins, installed to your computer, in order to display different features in the browser, including animated images, videos, and sound files.

PowerPoint. A presentation program developed by Microsoft. Provides the ability to integrate graphics and text and to display files in a format suitable for using as overheads, handouts, and speaker notes.

Shockwave. A popular browser plug-in used for viewing animated sequences. See *Macromedia Shockwave Player White Paper* for more information. Available: www.macromedia.com/software/shockwave player/whitepaper/.

URL. Uniform Resource Locator. The address for a Web page, or the address that you type into the "location" window of a Web browser to connect to Web pages or other sites on the Internet.

Web page. A single HTML document displayed by the Web browser.

Web site. A collection of organized Web pages, linked together.

WebQuest. An investigative activity designed by school media specialists and other teachers that encourages students to use information on the Web to answer a research question.

World Wide Web. A system, commonly known as the Web, for retrieving hypertext documents via the Internet. On the Web, documents are presented in HTML format and linked to other documents by their URLs.

ONLINE GLOSSARIES

Looking for the meaning of other Internet or computer terms, tools and topics? Try one of the following online glossaries or article directories, specializing in computer and Internet technology.

CNET—The Computer Network: Glossary
www.cnet.com/Resources/Info/Glossary/

HowStuffWorks—Computers and Internet
www.howstuffworks.com/sc-computers-internet.htm

TechWeb—TechEncyclopedia
www.techweb.com/encyclopedia/

Web Diner Glossary
www.webdiner.com/webadv/intro/glossary.htm

WhatIs.com—Definitions and references for current information technology words and topics.
http://whatis.techtarget.com/

Webmonkey Guides—Glossary of Terms
www.hotwired.lycos.com/webmonkey/guides/glossary/

Webopedia—Online Computer Dictionary for Internet Terms and Technical Support
www.webopedia.com/

Chapter Notes and References

CHAPTER 1—INSTRUCTIONAL PROGRAMS

Notes

American Library Association. 1999. *American Libraries: News for September 27, 1999. Chicago PL Internet Hits Are Less Than 5% Sexually Explicit* [Online]. Available: www.ala.org/alonline/news/1999/990927.html [11 October 2001].

Appleton Public Library. 2001. *School Age Programs* [Online]. Available: http://kids.apl.org/programs/school.html [9 October 2001].

Berry, John III. 1999. *Library Journal* [Online]. Available: www.libraryjournal.com/articles/views/editorial/19991001_11676.asp [11 October 2001].

Chicago Public Library. n.d. *Internet Use at CPL* [Online]. Available: www.chipublib.org/003cpl/internet/policy.html [2001, October 11].

The Children's Partnership. 1998. *The Parent's Guide to the Information Superhighway—When Is Your Child Ready?* [Online]. Available: www.childrenspartnership.org/pub/pbpg98/partI98.html#whenready [10 October 2001].

Family Friendly Libraries. 1999. *News and Views: Excellent Report by a Fellow Pro-Family Advocate* [Online]. Available: www.fflibraries.org/Newsletters/News_and_Views%201999.htm [11 October 2001].

Healy, Jane. 1998. *Failure to Connect: How Computers Affect Our Children's Minds—for Better and Worse.* New York: Simon & Schuster.

"Kids on the Keyboard: Keyboarding Milestones." 2001. *Children's Software Revue*. (May/June): 40–41.

King, Carol. 2001. College Knowledge Via the World Wide Web. *InternetNews* [Online]. Available: www.internetnews.com/ec-news/article/0,,4_584831,00.html [12 October 2001].

Minkel, Walter. 2001. Not So Elementary: How Young Is Too Young to Go Online? *School Library Journal* [Online]. Available: www.slj.com/articles/chatroom/20010101_9339.asp [10 October 2001].

Moyer, Kim. 2001. Clicking In To College: Online Administration. *Converge Magazine* [Online]. Available: www.convergemag.com/magazine/story.phtml?id=3030000000002943 [12 October 2001].

New York Public Library. 2000. *A Safety Net for the Internet: A Parent's Guide* [Online]. Available: www.nypl.org/branch/safety.html [9 October 2001].

Pew Internet and American Life Project. 2000. *Teens and Parents Survey: What Teens Have Done Online* [Online]. Available: www.pewinternet.org/reports/chart.asp?img=16_teen_activities.jpg [12 October 2001].

———. 2001. *Teen Life Online: The Internet Has a Pivotal Role in the Lives of Teenagers* [Online]. Available: www.pewinternet.org/reports/reports.asp?Report=36&Section=ReportLevel2&Field=Level2ID&ID=188 [12 October 2001].

Seattle Public Library Children's Services. 2001. *Internet Safety Links for Parents/Teachers* [Online]. Available: www.spl.org/children/safety.html [9 October 2001].

U.S. National Commission on Libraries and Information Science. 1999. *Kids and The Internet: The Promise and The Perils. Practical Guidelines for Librarians and Library Trustees* [Online]. Available: www.nclis.gov/info/kids2.html [29 September 2001].

References

American Library Association. 1999. *Librarian's Guide to Cyberspace for Parents and Kids* [Online]. Available: www.ala.org/parentspage/greatsites/guide.html [9 October 2001].

Coalition of America's Colleges and Universities. *College Is Possible* [Online]. Available: www.collegeispossible.org [12 October 2001].

Family Friendly Libraries [Online]. Available: www.fflibraries.org/index.htm and www.fflibraries.org/Welcome_Mat/pres.htm [11 October 2001].

Technology for Educational Achievement in Wisconsin [Online]. Available: www.teachwi.state.wi.us/ [12 October 2001].

U.S. Department of Education. *Think College* [Online]. Designed

to provide information on educational opportunities beyond high
school for learners of all ages. Available: www.ed.gov/thinkcollege/
[12 October 2001].

Additional Reading

Aftab, Perry. 2000. *The Parents Guide to Protecting Children in
Cyberspace.* New York: McGraw-Hill.

Coalition of America's Colleges and Universities. *College Is Possible*
[Online]. Available: www.collegeispossible.org. A guide to the
books, Web sites, and other resources that admissions and financial aid professionals consider most helpful in planning for college.

Family Friendly Libraries [Online]. Available: www.fflibraries.org/.
A nonprofit organization dedicated to "encouraging the appropriate and rightful role of citizens to influence local library policies,
particularly those affecting children."

Ginsberg, Mark. 2001. *Computers and Young Children* [Online].
National Association for the Education of Young Children. Available: www.naeyc.org/resources/eyly/2001/01.htm.

CHAPTER 2—CURRICULUM-RELATED PROGRAMS

Notes

Broch, Elena. 2000. Children's Search Engines from an Information
Search Process Perspective. *School Library Media Journal*
[Online]. Available: www.ala.org/aasl/SLMR/vol3/childrens/
childrens.html [6 October 2001].

Dodge, Bernie. 1997. *Some Thoughts About WebQuests* [Online].
Available: http://edweb.sdsu.edu/courses/edtec596/about_
webquests.html [6 October 2001].

———. *What's a WebQuest? Site Overview* [Online]. Available:
www.edweb.sdsu.edu/webquest/overview.htm [6 October 2001].

Ellerbee, Linda. 1999. *Girl Reporter Blows Lid Off Town!* New York:
Harper Trophy.

Minkel, Walter. 2000. "What Students Know Before They Go Online
Matters." *School Library Journal.* (August): 22.

Valenza, Joyce. 2000. *A WebQuest About School Library Web Sites*
[Online]. Available: http://mciu.org/~spjvweb/evallib.html [6 October 2001].

References

Knowledge Quest: *An Online Companion to the Journal of the American Association of School Librarians* [Online]. Available: www.ala.org/aasl/kqweb/ [6 October 2001].

Library of Congress. *American Memory Fellows Program* [Online]. Available: http://memory.loc.gov/ammem/ndlpedu/amfp/index.html [6 October 2001].

Multnomah County Public Library. *Homework Center Homework Help* [Online]. Available: www.multnomah.lib.or.us/lib/homework/ [6 October 2001].

Multnomah County Public Library. *Web Camp* [Online]. Available: www.webcamp2000.org/ [6 October 2001].

Additional Reading

American Library Association and Association for Educational Communications and Technology. 1998. *Information Power: The Nine Information Literacy Standards for Student Learning* [Online]. Available: www.ala.org/aasl/ip_nine.html [7 October 2001].

Green, Doug. 1997. The Web as a Tool for Research. *From Now On: The Educational Technology Journal* [Online]. Available: www.fno.org/jan97/websearch.html [7 October 2001].

Junion-Metz, Gail. 2001. *Coaching Kids for the Internet: A Guide for Librarians, Teachers, and Parents.* Berkeley, California: Library Solutions Press. Comprehensive manual provides explanation of Internet and Web searching tools. Appendices include lists of Web sites for learning more about teaching with the Web and for using with students. Excellent.

Lubans, John Jr. 1999. "When Students Hit the Surf: What Kids Really Do on the Internet and What They Want from Librarians." *School Library Journal* (September): 144-147. "Students also said they want us to develop finding aids to the Web—best site listing by subject. And they're looking for objective, informed suggestions about search engines, such as which work best under what circumstances." (p. 147).

McKenzie, Jamie. 1997. The Question Is the Answer. Creating Research Programs for an Age of Information. *From Now On: The Educational Technology Journal* [Online]. Available: www.fno.org/oct97/question.html [12 October 2001].

———. 1998. Learning Digitally. *From Now On: The Educational Technology Journal* [Online]. Available: www.fno.org/nov98/digital.html [7 October, 2001]

———. 2000. When the Book? When the Net? *From Now On: The Educational Technology Journal* [Online]. Available: www.fno.org/mar2000/whenbook.html [7 October 2001].

————. *questioning.org.* n.d. *A Focus on Questions and School Research. Nothing Else* [Online]. Available: www.questioning.org [12 October 2001].

Raskin, Robin. 2000. "Being Smart, Internet Style." *FamilyPC* (July): 61–63. "As we move to a world where knowledge resides online, the definition of a smart person may be different. The smart person in the '00s won't be the one who knows everything. She'll be the one who knows where to go to find what she needs" (p. 61).

Stokes, Peter J. 2000. How E-Learning Will Transform Education. *Education Week on the Web* [Online]. Available: www.edweek.org/ew/ewstory.cfm?slug=02stokes.h20 [14 October 2001].

CHAPTER 3: SUMMER READING PROGRAMS

Notes

American Library Association, Public Information Office. 1998. *Fact Sheet: Kids Who Read Succeed* [Online]. Available: www.ala.org/pio/factsheets/kidsucceed.html [30 September 2001].

Minkel, Walter. 2000. "Life's a Beach: Walter Minkel Tells You What You Need to Know to Plan a Summer Reading Web Site for 2001." *NetConnect*, supplement to *Library Journal* and *School Library Journal* (Fall): 42-43.

References

World Wide Web Consortium. 1999. *Checklist of Checkpoints for Web Content Accessibility Guidelines 1.0* [Online]. Available: www.w3.org/TR/1999/WAI-WEBCONTENT-19990505/full-checklist [4 October 2001].

CHAPTER 4—RECREATIONAL PROGRAMS

Notes

Harel, Idit. 2000. *Learning Skills for the Millennium: The Three X's* [Online]. MaMaMedia. Available: www.mamamedia.com/areas/grownups/new/21_learning/three_xs.html [12 October 2000].

————. 2000. *What Makes a Good Kids' Website?* [Online]. MaMaMedia. Available: www.mamamedia.com/areas/grownups/new/21_learning/good_kidsite.html [12 October 2000].

Mohawk Valley Library Association, NY. *I Spy—About the Project* [Online]. Available: www.mvla.org/ispy/about.html [14 October 2001].

References:

Bozeman (Montana) Public Library. *Bozeman Public Library* [Online]. Available: www.bozemanlibrary.org/ [14 October 2001].

Netscape. *Using Composer* [Online]. Available: http://help.netscape.com/products/client/communicator/IntroComm/chap05.html [14 October 2001].

Credits

In grateful acknowledgement to the following libraries and librarians for sharing information about their work and granting permission to reproduce selected images and reports.

Akron-Summit County Public Library, Ohio
www.ascpl.lib.oh.us
(Special thanks to Jan Chapman, young adult librarian, and her colleagues Becky Davis and Lori Mertel)

Bozeman Public Library, Montana
www.bozemanlibrary.org/
(Special thanks to Pam Henley, children's librarian)

Carmel Clay Public Library, Indiana
www.carmel.lib.in.us
(Special thanks to Jennifer Andersen, children's librarian)

Chicago Public Library, Illinois
www.chipublib.org/
(Special thanks to Cindy Welch, young adult specialist)

Daughin County Library System, Pennsylvania
www.dcls.org
(Special thanks to Dave Goudsward, Web administrator, and
Linda Moffet, assistant youth services coordinator)

The Ellis School, Pennsylvania
www.theellisschool.org/
(Special thanks to Kathy Koenig, director of libraries)

Heritage Middle School, New Jersey
www.heritage-ms.org/
(Special thanks to Librarian Alice Yucht)

Marlborough Public Library, Massachusetts
www.marlborough.com/library/index.html
(Special thanks to Susan Alatalo, young adult librarian)

Martin Library, York County Library System, Pennsylvania
www.yorklibraries.org/
(Special thanks to Margaret Ahrens, YCLS youth technology specialist)

Milwaukee Public Library, Wisconsin
www.mpl.org
(Special thanks to Leah Raven, grant project coordinator)

Monroe County Public Library, Indiana
www.monroe.lib.in.us
(Special thanks to Dana Burton, teen services manager)

Multnomah County Library, Oregon
www.multcolib.org
(Special thanks to Ellen Fader, youth services coordinator; Erica Moore, school corps librarian; and Jackie Partch, school corps team leader)

The Nueva School, California
www.nuevaschool.org/
(Special thanks to Librarian Debbie Abilock, curriculum, library, technology coordinator)

Ross Library, Pennsylvania
www.rosslibrary.org/
(Special thanks to Denise D. Selmer-Larsen, young adult librarian)

Springfield Township High School, Pennsylvania
www.springfield.k12.pa.us/shs/
(Special thanks to Librarian Joyce Valenza)

Timberland Regional Public Library, Washington
www.timberland.lib.wa.us

(Special thanks to Ellen Duffy, youth services coordinator, and Kristine Mahood and Tiffany Tuttle, youth service librarians)

Additional thanks to Librarians Carrie Gardner and Carolyn Noah for helping to spread the word!

Index

About the Author

Lisa Champelli worked as a writer and editor for an international service organization's magazine before returning to school to study library services to children and the Internet. She received both her bachelor's degree in journalism and her master's degree in library and information science from Indiana University, Bloomington. Since 1996 she has had the wonderful good fortune to work as a children's librarian with the children's services staff of Monroe County Public Library in Bloomington, Indiana, where she spends her days promoting good books and information literacy skills to inquisitive kids.

Coauthor of *Neal-Schuman WebMaster* (1997), Champelli develops and maintains MCPL's children's services Web site and conducts Web design workshops and other Internet programs for children. She is a member of the Indiana Library Federation's Intellectual Freedom Committee and has shared her experience in using the Web with young people at Indiana Library Federation and American Library Association conference programs.